Life of Jesus
IN CHRONOLOGICAL ORDER

MIKE MAZZALONGO

ISBN: 978-0-9904155-7-2

BibleTalk Books
14998 E. Reno
Choctaw, Oklahoma 73020

Scripture quotations taken from the New American Standard
Bible®, Copyright © 1960, 1962, 1963, 1968, 1971, 1972,
1973, 1975, 1977, 1995 by The Lockman Foundation Used by
permission. (www.Lockman.org

TABLE OF CONTENTS

INTRODUCTION

One of the more popular forms of books has been the biography of famous people. We love to read about the intimate details and early lives of the rich and famous or those who have made significant contributions to society. It seems that by reading about their lives, we measure our own. Many times we are inspired to change or try things because of the example of another. Biographies also give us insights into the forces and events that shaped the person and help us understand the world of the past and also how these influences shape our own lives. It would seem natural then that studying the life of Jesus would benefit us in all of these ways and also help establish a true standard for living since we are looking at the life of the Son of God.

Usually when we study the gospels, we are looking at the teachings of Jesus and what they mean and how they can be applied in our lives. We rarely study Jesus Himself, His life in the order He lived it. The reason for this is because the gospel writers each record a variety of incidents in Jesus' life not recorded by the others. So when you read the 4 gospels, one after another, you're not always sure how the events flow. They each tell the story from His birth to His death, but the details in between are not always explained in chronological order so you can get a sense of how one event leads to another.

This book therefore will have several objectives:

- I will present to you the life of Jesus in chronological order. What He did and where He went from first to last in a step-by-step description.

- Help you prepare a notebook where you will have:

  - The events in Jesus' life listed in order.

  - Parallel scriptural references for these events also listed in chronological order.

- For this I would ask you to get a notebook, preferably one that will hold 8½ by 11 inch paper (ring binder).

  - For example your notes will look like this. A template can be downloaded at **bibletalk.tv/life-of-jesus-events**

#	Event/Comment	Mt.	Mk.	Lk.	Jn.

By the end of this course you will have a notebook with a complete biography of Jesus' life, ministry, miracles and passion all listed in chronological order.

Jesus' Ministry

When Jesus was born the world kept time according to the Roman calendar. The Roman calendar was based on the year that the city of Rome was founded. With this calculation, Jesus was born in the year 735 because the city of Rome was said to have been founded 735 years previous to the year of His birth, so if we kept with this calendar we'd be in the year 2746 Roman time as of the year 2014.

Some people of that era kept time according to the years a certain king or emperor was in power – IE Luke 3:1, John's ministry is said to begin in the 15th year of the reign of Tiberius Caesar.

In the Middle Ages the Christian calendar was introduced using the birth of Jesus as the zero point. When calculations were made and calendars produced and distributed it was noted that an error was made and that the date of Jesus' birth was actually 4 years before the zero date they had previously calculated. Since all had been done, they left it alone. This is how it came to be that when pinpointing the calendar date of Jesus' birth, scholars tell us that He was born in 4 BC!

We also know that He died when He was 33. Luke 3:23 says He was 30 years of age when He began His ministry. When you review His ministry event by event you see that He lived through 3 annual Passover celebrations and died during the celebration of the 4th.

If He was born around 4 BC and died at 33, it means the calendar date of His death is approximately 29 AD – so Pentecost happened in 29 AD. Those churches whose cornerstone says, "This church established in 33 AD" have the right doctrine and spirit, but they have the wrong date.

Even by New Testament standards, 33 was still young to die. The normal life span was about 50-55 years at that time.

When studying Jesus' life we can divide it into 7 main periods:

1. Jesus' Boyhood – 0-12 years

These include incidents and prophecies that led to His birth and the little information we have about His childhood.

There have been many books written about this time that show Jesus doing miracles (stretching lumber for Joseph) or living with the desert monks (Essenes) where He was trained, but these are based on fables and stories circulated about His life in the early years. The only information God has revealed about His childhood is limited and contained in a few passages of Matthew and Luke.

2. Inauguration of Jesus' Public Ministry

At the age of thirty, Jesus leaves His obscure life in Nazareth and Capernaum in the northern region and travels south to begin His public ministry. This debut is spectacular and includes His meeting with John the Baptist.

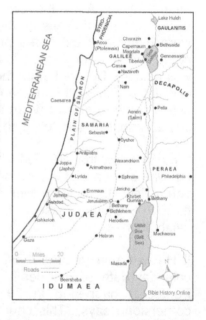

3. Public Ministry of Jesus from 1st to 2nd Passover

Most of the information for this period is found in the book of John. Jesus performs most of His ministry in Jerusalem and departs for the north.

4. Public Ministry of Jesus from 2nd to 3rd Passover

Thirty six events make up this section where most of the action takes place in Galilee, the northern part of the country where Jesus originally grew up.

5. Ministry from the 3rd Passover to the Beginning of the Last Passover Week

This is the longest section in the New Testament. There are 61 events mentioned in this period and all 4 writers describe these in detail. During this time we see Jesus going back and forth from the north, northwest to the southern capital of Jerusalem.

This section also describes some of the stays along the way where Jesus carried out His ministry walking to and fro with disciples accompanying Him on the road.

6. Last Passover Week Ending with Crucifixion

We will go through this section giving you the events day by day as they took place. According to our present day calendars, it would have been Sunday, April 2nd to Saturday, April 7th, His final day in the tomb.

7. Resurrection, Appearances and Ascension

Aside from His ascension before the Apostles, the Bible counts 10 separate appearances to more than 540 people in a space of 40 days. We will go over these in our study.

Hopefully at the end of our study the ministry of Jesus, His life and His work will become more real, more understandable as a historical event and not simply a string of teachings gathered together in 4 books.

In each chapter I'll try to focus in on some event or teaching to draw a lesson or share a word of encouragement.

Lessons

In this chapter we've not looked at any one event, but rather an overview of Jesus' movements and work. However, even this brief review provides several important lessons:

1. There was a Method

When you read the gospels you don't readily see the pattern of His movements, but there definitely was a well-laid plan.

A. Early years at home with family.

B. The announcement of His ministry in the southern capital where John was, along with the Jewish leaders and the bulk of the population.

C. Return to the north to actually begin His teaching and miracles for His own family, recruiting His own neighbors as disciples.

D. Returning to Jerusalem to expand His ministry once it was established.

E. Spending time in the north and after being rejected and hunted by leaders in the capital.

F. Final appearance in Jerusalem which resulted in His death and resurrection. Church begins in Jerusalem and spreads out.

2. Movements Based on Prophecy

The fact that He was born in Bethlehem and raised in Nazareth were mentioned in the prophets (Micah 5:2; Matthew 2:23 respectively).

Jesus Himself mentioned that He did the will of the Father. The Holy Spirit moved Him to go into the desert to be tempted. He did not go to Jerusalem until the "time" was fulfilled.

So we don't see mindless wandering, but rather a well ordered ministry timed to be in certain places at certain periods based on God's word in the prophets and His will during the period Jesus was physically on earth.

3. Small Area – Great Impact

Jesus covered a corridor roughly 100 miles long and 60 miles wide in His 3 year ministry. Look at the impact over 2,000 years later. When we are thinking we can't do much for Christ from our little town or our small resources, remember how much came from so little.

If God directs our work and efforts, we can affect the world for Christ from right where we live.

READING ASSIGNMENT FOR CHAPTER 2

1. Luke 1:1-4; John 1:1-18

2. Matthew 1:1-17; Luke 3:23-38

3. Luke 1:5-25

4. Luke 1:26-38

5. Luke 1:39-56

6. Luke 1:57-80

7. Matthew 1:18-25

8. Luke 2:1-7

9. Luke 2:8-20

10. Luke 2:21-38

11. Matthew 2:1-12

12. Matthew 2:13-15

13. Matthew 2:16-18

14. Matthew 2:19-23; Luke 2:39-40

15. Luke 2:41-52

2.
BOYHOOD

This chapter will attempt to review the life of Jesus in chronological order fitting all the events into sequence. In the last chapter we looked at an overview of the 7 major periods in His life. In this chapter we will begin by outlining the information dealing with the period of His youth. Hopefully you have used the reading guide to read ahead.

1. Introduction

Luke 1:1-4; John 1:1-18

Luke's gospel is the only one that implies that it was written as a letter and so the introduction explains the reason for the letter. Luke's gospel is the most historical in nature and contains the most details (119 of the total 154 events are described in Luke).

John's prologue (In the beginning was the Word...) announced the theme of his gospel. This is different from Luke in that it isn't a letter, different from the others in that Matthew and Mark begin by telling the story from the very beginning of their books. John's first 18 verses summarizes the life and purpose of Christ and defines His nature and source from the very outset of the book – then in verse 19 he goes on to tell the story beginning with John's preaching.

2. The Genealogies

Matthew 1:1-17; Luke 3:23-38

Before any action or personalities are introduced, the genealogy of Jesus is given in order to establish several things:

- His place within the Jewish community – You were a Jew because you belonged to the nation and your place in the nation was confirmed and maintained in the records of the families and their descendants (written records).

- His direct relationship to David – The prophets told that the Messiah would be a descendant of David from the tribe of Judah. Anyone claiming to be the Messiah would have to be within this lineage.

Matthew's genealogy describes Jesus' royal genealogy tracing it from Abraham to David to Joseph and thus His legal authority to claim the title of Messiah. Luke describes His natural descendance from Adam. They are different because the authors choose different people on the list of descendants to mention in order to make their case.

For example, from Adam to Joseph there were 300 descendants (an arbitrary number used for the sake of this example), each mentions different ones (Matthew: Abraham, #103, #107, #208, #286, etc. until he gets to #300: Joseph). Luke does it in reverse (#300: Joseph, #297, #295, #161, #142, until he gets to Adam: #1).

Genealogies are there to show that Jesus was a Jew and had a legitimate claim to the rule of Messiah according to Prophets who said the Messiah would come through David's lineage. After the destruction of Jerusalem all the genealogies and records were destroyed, and the only record actually kept is the one of Jesus.

3. Announcement of John's birth

Luke 1:5-25

A priest named Zacharias married to a woman named Elizabeth who is the cousin of Mary of Nazareth, he is chosen by lot (once in a lifetime privilege) to burn incense on the altar in the court of the priests just in front of the holy of Holies (where only the High Priest was allowed to enter once per year). While doing this an angel appears to tell him that his wife will have a son (she had been barren and now past child bearing). He doubted and was struck dumb until the child was born.

4. Birth of Jesus announced

Luke 1:26-38

Six months after John's birth is announced, Jesus' birth is announced, but this time to the woman who would bear the child, Mary of Nazareth. The angel tells her that unlike John who would be great in the sight of the Lord, a perpetual Nazarite (no meat or alcohol), a servant of God (why Nazarite), and filled with the Holy Spirit. Mary's son would be conceived by supernatural means and He would be the long awaited Messiah. Both would have missions: one would prepare the way for the other; one would announce and introduce and the other would fulfill all said about Him in prophecy.

5. Mary visits Elizabeth

Luke 1:39-56

In the last three months of Elizabeth's pregnancy and during the first three months of her own, Mary visits her elderly cousin and assists in her final months of pregnancy. When they meet, Mary pronounces a beautiful poem, called the "Magnificat" by many scholars. In the poem she praises God for His goodness to her (the honor of being the mother of the Messiah), His kindness to all who fear Him, His help to those who are oppressed (sending the Messiah), and her peace and joy at her condition. The entire poem is taken from various passages in the Old Testament showing Mary's knowledge of the Word.

6. John the Baptist's birth

Luke 1:57-80

John is born soon after Mary's departure and his name is given as John (a surprise because no one in Zacharias' family has this name). Zacharias agreed with the name (given by an angel) and receives back his speech. When he does he begins praising God (he too with references from the Old Testament).

7. The angel appears to Joseph

Matthew 1:18-25

Matthew tells the story from Joseph's perspective, Luke from Mary's. They were betrothed meaning that the dowry was set, the commitment to marry was done, the house was chosen – all that was left was the wedding feast (usually 1 year after betrothal) and moving into the home. Before the wedding feast and consummation, Mary becomes pregnant by the Holy Spirit. Some doubt this and deny it using several arguments:

- They say that this part was added later by unknown, uninspired writers.
- They claim that virgin birth was not held by the early church because epistles don't write about it.
- Impossible naturally (don't believe in miracles).

Of course the answer to this is that both Matthew and Luke mention quite specifically the fact that Mary conceived in a miraculous fashion – just like they both mention that Jesus resurrected in a miraculous fashion. One is not more difficult for God than the other.

Joseph is also told by an angel that Mary has conceived by the power of God, he will name the child Jesus (Greek form of Hebrew name Joshua which means "the Lord is salvation"), and his son will be the Messiah.

Like Mary, Joseph believed the angel and followed through in obedience. She accepted to be pregnant and had the baby. He accepted her pregnancy and prepared to be the father by providing her his name and a home to live in.

Matthew 1:25 says that he "kept" her a virgin until she had a son. This means that after she had Jesus he no longer kept her a virgin and this explains the sons and daughters spoken of in other passages (at least 4 brothers and 2 sisters). Mark 6:3 says that Jesus was the oldest of 7.

8. Birth of Jesus

Luke 2:1-7

It is interesting to note that the world places so much importance on the birth of Jesus, but only one writer describes it. Jesus was conceived while Mary was betrothed to Joseph (legally married but not yet living together). He was born in Bethlehem, the city of David, according to prophecy (Micah 5:2). The actual giving of names in long distance prophecy is very rare, but Micah actually gives the name of the city where the Messiah will be born. The reason, historically, was that there was a census and you had to go to your native city to be counted. Joseph was of the house of David and probably owned a small plot of land there so he had to be there for the counting.

9. Angels announce His birth

Luke 2:8-20

Historians tell us that shepherds had their flocks out grazing between March and November, so the time of Jesus' birth is somewhere in this period. That shepherds are the first to know is unusual: they were poor and unimportant, they were not part of religious establishment but they were symbolic of the type of Messiah Jesus was and representative of the nation of Israel. The shepherds represent those who come and worship the new Messiah from His people.

10. Circumcision of Jesus

Luke 2:21-38

Being devout Jews, Mary and Joseph have Jesus circumcised. This was eight days after His birth. A month later, they returned (33 days) for a purification rite (could offer 2 turtledoves if too poor to offer a lamb, which is what they did). It was at this time that Simeon and Anna, two elderly prophet and prophetess who spoke concerning Jesus' future and confirmed that this child was truly the Messiah. This was done to confirm and encourage Joseph and Mary who were the only ones to hear this prophecy.

11. Visit of the Magi

Matthew 2:1-12

Tradition shows the Magi showing up at the manger on the heels of the shepherds – this is incorrect. Matthew 2:16 says that Herod killed children two and under according to how old the child was based on the information given him by the Magi. Putting the verses together we get this possible order of events:

- They leave Nazareth to go to Bethlehem
- Jesus is born there
- They go to Jerusalem 8 days later for circumcision
- They return to Nazareth to pack up

- They go to Jerusalem for Purification (1 month)
- They settle in Bethlehem because since it is the city of David, city of the Messiah, this is where they believe they should raise Jesus

After a year or so the Magi arrive looking for the Messiah according to the star they had seen. Matthew 2:11 says that they came to a house in Bethlehem where Joseph and Mary had settled. They didn't come to a manger as the pictures and traditions indicate. Jesus has been announced to the Jews (through the shepherds) and the Gentiles (through the Magi). Magi were astrologers and counselors to the king in Babylon.

12. Flight into Egypt

Matthew 2:13-15

Jesus' life and movements were dictated by the prophets' words concerning Him. Hosea 11:1 speaks of the Nation of Israel and their experience in Egypt when he says "out of Egypt I will call my son." Matthew takes this passage and applies it to Jesus as He is embodying the Jewish nation's experience in His own lifetime as He also is forced to live in Egypt for a time. Joseph is warned that Herod will try to destroy the Messiah and told to flee to Egypt. They could have fled to any town, but in order for Scripture to be fulfilled they had to go to Egypt.

The gospel writers used the Old Testament scriptures to suit their purposes. Even if the prophet's words did not specifically state something in context, the gospel writers would use their words to express certain ideas regardless of context. This was the liberty of inspiration – God created the proper context and meaning using the same words to express different things.

Their move to Egypt was probably financed by the gold and precious ointments brought by the Magi. Mary and Joseph were poor and God provided for their needs.

13. Herod's murder of innocents

Matthew 2:16-18

Soon after their escape Herod tried to eliminate a seeming threat to his throne (he didn't understand) by killing all males under 2. This was Jesus' maximum age according to the Magi's account. Herod died in 4 BC so this is why we say that Jesus was born between 7-4 BC. Probably a year old when He was taken to Egypt, stayed there about a year and when Herod died in 4 BC Joseph and Mary return then.

14. Return to Nazareth

Matthew 2:19-23; Luke 2:39-40

Joseph and Mary had tried to settle in Bethlehem thinking this is where the Messiah should be raised so they try to return there after hiding out in Egypt. God informs him that Herod is dead and he can return to Israel. When he realizes that Herod's son is reigning in the area where he wants to return (Bethlehem), he is told to go back to his original home – Nazareth. Nazareth was in a region further from Herod's headquarters and not one where people expected the Messiah to come from. It was the city that the prophets said the Messiah would *emerge* from but not be born in – Matthew 2:23. This was a subtle difference that only revelation could provide.

15. Twelve year old Jesus in Jerusalem

Luke 2:41-52

Jews were required to go to the Temple for all the feasts, but by the 1st century this had dropped to one per year – the feast of the Passover. Jewish boys reached accountability at thirteen (a son of the commandment). Many boys went to the temple at even earlier ages as was the case with Jesus.

The Rabbis would often find large crowds to teach at these times. His parents lose sight of Jesus and find Him in one such group discussing the Law, asking and answering questions of them. His reply to his mother when they found Him, "Did you not know that I had to be in my Father's house" shows that He was already, at 12, aware of His divine nature and mission. These are His first recorded words.

After this event there is silence concerning Jesus' early life until the beginning of His ministry at 30. All we know is that he remained with His parents in Nazareth and served as a dutiful son until His public ministry began.

Lessons

This part gives us little information about Jesus but a great deal about His parents.

1. They were true believers.

Their faith cost them something and yet they continued to believe. There is no faith without risk – if it's a sure thing then there is no faith.

2. They believed despite their lack of understanding.

They continued to believe even though the events were unfolding around them. We believe based on a complete story. They didn't know the end but trusted the Lord day by day. Some things in our life are like that, we need to trust and obey even though things aren't fully worked out yet.

26

READING ASSIGNMENT FOR CHAPTER 3

16. Matthew 3:1-12; Mark 1:1-8; Luke 3:1-18; John 1:28

17. Matthew 3:13-17; Mark 1:9-11; Luke 3:21-23

18. Matthew 4:11; Mark 1:12-13; Luke 4:1-13

19. John 1:15-34

20. John 1:35-42

21. John 1:43-51

22. John 2:1-12

28

3.
BEGINNING OF MINISTRY

In the last chapter we began with the first major section of Jesus' life – the period from just before His birth to a time when He was twelve years old.

There is much speculation about the period after this until His 30th year, but the Bible simply states that He returned to be with His parents.

Since the Bible states that His turning water into wine was His first miracle performed and subsequent visits to teach at His hometown synagogue was met with surprise, we can conclude a few things about this period:

1. He did not perform miracles and use His divine powers during this period.

2. He did not teach or proclaim His person or mission before this time, but simply attended and participated in worship like His fellow Jews.

3. He moved out from His family's home and headed for Jerusalem at the age of thirty.

His obscure life came to an end however when His ministry to the Jews began at the river Jordan with His cousin, John the Baptist.

Beginning of Public Ministry

There are seven events in this section on the beginning of Jesus' public ministry. These follow the first 15 events we've discussed so far.

16. The preaching of John the Baptist

Matthew 3:1-12; Mark 1:1-8; Luke 3:1-18; John 1:28

In their discussion of the future Messiah, the Old Testament prophets described a person who would appear on the scene as a forerunner to introduce or prepare the way for the Messiah (Isaiah 40:3; Malachi 3:1). With his appearance and preaching, John fulfilled this prophecy. John's message was twofold:

A. Repent of your sins and be baptized in order to symbolize the cleansing of your souls and the coming of the kingdom of God.

B. His successor would come to baptize these people not with water but with the Holy Spirit.

His preaching was accepted by two groups and rejected by two groups:

A. Those who recognized their sinfulness saw a chance to be right with God (even pagan soldiers).

B. Those who were anxiously awaiting the coming of the Messiah saw in John the one who was preparing His way.

C. Those who felt confident in their Jewish heritage and rejected any call to change.

D. Those who loved their sins refused to believe, especially in a Jewish Messiah.

Whatever the response, John got the nation's attention concerning the coming of the Lord.

17. The baptism of Jesus

Matthew 3:13-17; Mark 1:9-11; Luke 3:21-23

Baptism was a familiar religious rite among the Jews. The priests would wash completely before becoming priests or before putting on ceremonial robes. New converts to Judaism were required to be cleansed with water in addition to being circumcised and offering sacrifice at the temple.

We know John baptized with water and by immersion because the Jews required a cleansing of the entire body in their purification rites. Like circumcision, John's baptism was an expression of faith in response to God's offer. In circumcision the offer was to be counted among God's people. In John's baptism the offer was to have one's sins forgiven. Later in Jesus' baptism it was the triple offer of forgiveness of sins, the indwelling of the Holy Spirit and entry into the church.

Jesus signals the beginning of His ministry by accepting to be baptized by John. Why?

1. To fulfill all righteousness (Matthew 3:15). To respond to God's command with obedience.

2. To identify with sin – Jesus had no sins Himself but He took on the sins of others so with this act He acknowledges sin, He identifies with sinners.

3. To separate Himself from His old life. Baptism signifies death (Romans 6:3), separation of the spirit and the flesh. Jesus at age thirty is separating Himself from His old life of submission and obscurity and taking up

his new life of public ministry, Lordship and finally death and resurrection.

4. To fulfill prophecy (Isaiah 11:1-2, the dove; Isaiah 42:1, the voice). The prophet said the Messiah would have the Spirit on Him (11:1-2) and would be pleasing to God (42:1).

This new life, this inauguration of His public ministry is confirmed and witnessed by God in two ways:

1. **The heavens open and the Holy Spirit appears as a dove.** This shows that Jesus received the gift of the Holy Spirit at this time, as it came and rested upon Him. In His divine nature He was equal and similar to the Father and Holy Spirit, however His human nature received the gift of the Holy Spirit in order to enable Him to carry on His ministry.

2. **God the Father speaks to confirm that Jesus is indeed the divine Son and the one who is sent (Messiah).**

This is the only time in the Bible that there is a physical manifestation of the Trinity (Father/voice; Son/Jesus; Holy Spirit/dove). Also, this scene is a strong example for those who reject the "Trinity" idea in the Bible (IE. Jews, Muslims, Jehovah Witnesses).

18. Jesus is tempted in the desert

Matthew 4:11; Mark 1:12-13; Luke 4:1-13

Satan tempts Jesus while He is fasting in the desert. The word tempt can mean to "test" or "examine" rather than appeal to some lust or evil. Since Jesus had no sin, the devil's "test" was to create sin in Him in some way.

- He tempts Jesus to pride by asking Him to do a miracle to prove His lordship. (Making the stones bread.)
- He tempts Jesus to idolatry by offering Him something in exchange for worship. (All kingdoms of the earth if He would worship him.)
- He tempts Jesus to presumptuousness by asking Him to test God. (Throw Himself down from the tower to see if God will save Him.)

The Father had already given Jesus all of these things. He called Him the beloved son, no need to confirm this with a miracle. The Father had already promised everything to His Son (Psalm 2:8). Satan was offering something that wasn't his to give. The Father had promised in the word (quoted by Satan) that He would care for the Son, no need to test God's word for accuracy.

After this event, the angels minister to the Lord.

19. John's witness concerning Jesus

John 1:15-34

John's gospel provides a detailed summary of John's preaching and the reaction of the people, especially the leaders. John 1:15 shows that the Baptist was aware of and preached that he was preparing the way for the Messiah. There is no ambiguity – it was a clear message. John testified about Him and cried out, saying,

This was He of whom I said, 'He who comes after me has a higher rank than I, for He existed before me.'
- John 1:15

This also shows that he shared in the experience of the voice of the Father and the settling of the dove. This was the way that John knew that Jesus was indeed the one. He had an impact on the people because even the leaders were curious about who he was. Some thought he was the Christ. Some thought he was Elijah. Some thought he was Moses (people believed that the great prophet Moses would resurrect at the coming of the Messiah). John denies all of these and responds that he is simply a "voice" sent to prepare the way.

20. Jesus' first Apostles

John 1:35-42

John has introduced Him and also encourages his own disciples to follow after Jesus. The Lord did not select all of His Apostles in one day or week. They came in twos and threes over a period of months. Some, like Peter, began to follow Jesus while still maintaining his fishing business, but after a while Jesus called him into full time ministry and he left all to follow the Lord. In this event Andrew calls his brother Simon to come and meet Jesus – the one whom he believes to be the Messiah. It is during this first meeting that Jesus gives Simon a new name – Peter.

21. More disciples in Galilee

John 1:43-51

Andrew and Peter were probably in the region to hear John preach and that's how they meet Jesus. After their meeting (in Jerusalem area) Jesus returns up north to the area of Galilee around where He grew up, and where Peter and Andrew come from. While He is there John says that He finds Philip and in turn Philip finds Nathaniel. These men initially follow Jesus because they believe that He is the Messiah (Nathaniel says so after Jesus reveals something about him that no one else could know). At this point their concept of what the Messiah is supposed to be is not fully developed, but Jesus through His miracles, teachings and especially His resurrection will open their eyes and hearts.

22. First miracle at Cana

John 2:1-12

It is interesting that John is the one filling in the details of this early part of Jesus' ministry since, as the cousin of Jesus (His mother Salome was Mary's sister), and as one who was included in Jesus' inner circle, he had access to the early information within the family and was probably present at many of these early events. His family relationship to Jesus also explains why he was given the care of Mary and not Peter.

John describes a wedding feast taking place in Cana which is in the northern country just west of the Sea of Galilee. Jesus was there with His family including His disciples, many of whom were related to Jesus and each other.

There is a question about Mary's attitude concerning what Jesus was to do to intervene when the wine ran out. She was confident that Jesus could do something and goes to Him for help. Jesus responds that His hour has not come in the sense that it isn't time to be fully glorified (His death, burial, resurrection). What He says to her is that the matter is not her concern but His. If He does something it will be directed of the Father and not by the pleading of His mother. And so we see Mary understand that He will do something, but only because it is given by God and not her – and she prepares the servants to follow His instructions in anticipation of His actions.

Jesus transforms water into wine and launches the miraculous portion of His ministry within the circle of His own family, friends, disciples and region. John says that at this point His disciples believed in Him. After the wedding feast Jesus, Mary, His brothers and His disciples return to Capernaum (other side of the lake) to Jesus' home.

John makes a distinction between Jesus' brothers and His disciples. At this early time His brothers were not His disciples.

This is the end of His first northern or, Galilean, ministry. In the next chapter we will see Jesus leave the north and head towards Jerusalem again for His first public ministry appearance there.

Lessons

We can draw some practical lessons from these events in Jesus' life, especially in the area of evangelism. We see some ways that Jesus drew people to Himself, ways that are still relevant and possible today:

1. Preach Jesus as Lord

The first thing Jesus did was to demonstrate who He was by the witness of the Holy Spirit and the Father. Today, the first thing we should establish in any study, debate or teaching is that Jesus is the divine Son of God. If this point is made, all the others will flow from it – if not, then it doesn't matter.

2. The importance of obedience

The Bible is not for discussing, it's for obeying. We study and teach it in order to produce obedience. Jesus, in baptism and in the desert, showed that His Holiness was proven by His obedience to the Father. God not only wants us to hear the good news, He wants us to obey it and when we teach others we should be leading them to obedience.

3. Start at home

Jesus' first followers and disciples were family members, people from His town and region. Saving the world begins by saving yourself, your family, your neighbor, your buddy, etc. Effective evangelism is not about programs or projects, it's about people sharing with the people close to them.

READING ASSIGNMENT FOR CHAPTER 4

23. John 2:13-25

24. John 3:1-2

25. John 3:22-23

26. John 3:24-36

27. Luke 3:19-20

28. Matthew 11:2-19; Luke 7:18-35

29. Matthew 14:1-12; Mark 6:14-29; Luke 9:7-9

30. John 4:4-42

31. Matthew 4:17; Mark 1:14-15; Luke 4:14-15; John 4:43-45

32. John 4:46-54

4.
1st TO 2nd PASSOVER

So far we've covered 22 of the approximately 154 events of Jesus' life in chronological order. The last chapter reviewed what Jesus did during His early ministry around the northern area of Galilee where He was raised. In this chapter we begin with Jesus' appearance in Jerusalem and watch as His ministry starts to build momentum.

23. Jesus cleanses the temple

John 2:13-25

The first glimpse we have of Jesus as a young boy is when He is at the temple discussing the Law with the scribes and Pharisees. He was concerned about "My Father's house" at that time, but as a boy, remained in subjection to His parents and elders and leaders.

As a man, however, He still has a zeal for the Father's house but now expresses it in a much more dynamic way since He has begun His public ministry.

There is a debate whether or not there is one or two "cleansings" of the temple. John puts this incident at the beginning of Jesus' ministry and Matthew, Mark and Luke put it at the point where Jesus enters Jerusalem triumphantly and goes directly to the temple to do this. There are good arguments on both sides – my own view is that if John put it at the beginning and Matthew, Mark and Luke put it at the end; there were two similar incidents. This would be like the two incidents where Jesus performed the miracle of multiplying the bread and the fish. If He did this miracle twice, why not two cleansings? There was more than one miracle, more than one sermon; there could easily be more than one cleansing. Both times however, the reasons were similar for Jesus' actions in cleansing the Temple:

1. Violation of the Law

The Jews were selling animals and exchanging money in the court of the Gentiles. This desecrated the place where the Gentiles came to worship. The temple had a series of courtyards where people prayed, offered sacrifices and received teaching. The most inner courtyards were reserved for the priests, then as they extended outward there was a courtyard for Jewish men, another separate one for Jewish women and finally, the furthest out was one where Gentiles who had converted to Judaism or sympathetic to the Jewish religion could go. The money-changers and herdsmen set up their tables there in order to service the worshippers who bought animals, thus ruining their worship and place to gather. This was blatant discrimination and disobedience.

Jesus creates quite a stir by making a whip out of cords and driving out the money-changers, herders and animals out of the temple area. This is done as a sign that the temple was meant to be pure and holy in every section.

2. He also did this to establish the idea that the temple as magnificent as it was, would one day be destroyed and a new temple, His body (the church), would be established.

The Messiah comes to His house and finds it unprepared for His sudden arrival.

This is the "type" for all the parables that speak of the judgment to come. It is also a living prophecy for the Jews (their judgment is at hand), and also for Christians today

(Jesus can come at any time). The issue for us is the same as it was for them, "Will we be ready when Jesus comes?"

During this explosive time He also teaches and performs miracles and begins to draw His first disciples from the area of Jerusalem.

24. A visit from Nicodemus

John 3:1-21

It is natural that His tumultuous arrival at the temple, His signs and His teachings would draw the interest of not only the crowds, but also the religious leaders. At the temple some leaders were questioning His right to do what He did and wondered what He meant by the idea that His "temple" would be raised in three days if it was destroyed. They saw Him as a troublemaker and wanted Him silenced.

Some, however, like Nicodemus came to Him secretly to learn more. Nicodemus knew He was special, but was slow to come to faith. Jesus showed him that even he, a teacher and scholar, required the "new birth" in order to enter the kingdom. John's baptism was for everyone. Nicodemus didn't understand at first. Later on, however, we see him trying to defend the Lord when the Jewish leaders were accusing Him unjustly. Finally, at Jesus' death, he provided the costly spices to properly bury Him. Nicodemus was a slow and cautious disciple, but he eventually came around.

25. Jesus returns to northern Judea

John 3:22-23

After this dynamic appearance, Jesus travels back to Samaritan territory in the northern part of Judea to work with John who was there preaching and baptizing.

For a short period their work overlapped. Note on the map (in the first chapter of this book) that they worked at the Jordan River in the Aenon region.

Jesus Himself did not baptize, but His disciples did as He preached. For a time their message (John and Jesus) was the same, "Repent and be baptized for the kingdom of heaven is at hand."

26. John's second witness

John 3:24-36

At the beginning, John points to Christ as He is revealed by the Father and Holy Spirit. While near Jerusalem he then encourages his disciples to follow Jesus.

Now that they are working in north Judea, side-by-side, John's disciples notice that Jesus is baptizing more people than John. They question him about this. John answers them by acknowledging that the purpose of his ministry was to prepare the way for Jesus' ministry and that it is proper that Jesus' ministry grows and his diminishes. John knew and rejoiced to see Jesus arrive and do what He was supposed to do. John happily accepted his lessor role. At this point he knew that he had succeeded in his mission - but later on he would doubt.

27. John's imprisonment

Luke 3:19-20

John was a preacher of judgment to come. The theme of his preaching was "repent" and so much of his sermons had to do with sin and the disobedience of the people. He didn't talk about the church or love of the brethren or other issues, he was a one topic preacher.

His preaching stepped on everyone's toes. He addressed the common man, the Roman soldiers, prostitutes, businessmen, even religious leaders and their sins. He got into trouble when he meddled in the affairs of the king. Herod had stolen his brother's wife and divorced his own to marry her (she was his niece). John publicly declared that this was against the Law and Herod needed to repent. This caused embarrassment to Herod and his wife, Herodias. John's continued accusation would lessen their position with the people (which wasn't very good to begin with). In order to silence him and stop him from stirring up the bad publicity, Herod had him put into prison.

28. John's inquiry of Jesus

Matthew 11:2-19; Luke 7:18-35

John the Baptist believed that the Messiah he was preparing the way for would come and usher in a great period of judgment and prosperity for the Jews. His "view" of the kingdom may have been similar to his fellow Jews of the time.

As a prophet, and like most prophets, he knew the order and general nature of the things he prophesied about in the future, but not necessarily the time frame.

- First he comes to prepare the way.
- Next the Messiah comes with spirit and power.
- Then a judgment comes on the people.
- Then a period of blessing (kingdom).

What he didn't know was how far apart these things would be in time and the exact nature of each of these events. He sees and recognizes the Messiah according to the signs God provided him in order to confirm his preaching. Then he witnesses the growth of his ministry and the number of people who begin to follow Him.

But now he's arrested and put into prison – no judgment comes down on the evil king. As a matter of fact, nothing in the "big picture" changes.

When neither judgment nor a great new order of things appears right away, John begins to doubt. He had the sequence right, but the time frame was wrong. Just like the Thessalonians who assumed that Jesus was returning in their lifetime and became distressed when this didn't happen.

At this point John sends his disciples to question Jesus. He thinks maybe that he's made a mistake and Jesus isn't the one since his concept of what was supposed to happen didn't materialize. There are many people like that, if their lives don't work out like they think it should, they begin to question and doubt God.

John sends his disciples to ask Jesus, "Are you the One or should we look for another?" Jesus replies that He was doing all the things the Scripture said that the Messiah would do when He came: teach, heal, raise the dead. These were the signs given to create faith in those seeking the Messiah, and John should trust in these (not his idea of how things should be).

Then Jesus rebukes those who rejected John because of his appearance and what happened to him.

29. John's death

Matthew 14:1-12; Mark 6:14-29; Luke 9:7-9

Three of four writers record John's death at the hands of Herod. Herod had an interesting relationship with John:

- As part Jew, he was familiar with the Jewish religion and recognized John as a powerful preacher and righteous man.
- He was naturally drawn to him.
- He kept John in prison for a time and would bring him to hear him preach in private.

He was also a worldly man as well as a shrewd politician and ruthless leader so he was in great conflict about what he should do with John.

His wife sensed this and ultimately tricked him into executing John in order to save face. When Jesus hears about John's death, He leaves the area of Judea He was working in and returns home to Galilee, a safer and friendlier place for the time being.

30. The Samaritan woman

John 4:4-42

We know that He was in Samaritan territory, baptizing with John. John is taken away and killed.

During this period, on His way home, he meets a Samaritan woman at a well and speaks with her. She is not only a Samaritan despised by the Jews, she is also a much divorced woman who is living with her boyfriend which makes her not much liked by the Samaritans either.

Jesus reveals His true person to her by knowing her past and by showing her kindness in spite of it. His acceptance of her and His answers to her questions win her over and she, the outcast, gains the courage to go tell her neighbors and friends about Jesus. We find out that because of this He stays extra days in the area (delaying His return) in order to teach and preach to these people.

31. Public ministry in Galilee

Matthew 4:17; Mark 1:14-15; Luke 4:14-15; John 4:43-45

After He finishes in Samaria the writers tell us that He returned to His home region and officially begins His public ministry there. Before, with the calling of disciples and miracle at Cana, He was still acting privately among family and friends.

Once John has died, Jesus goes home and begins there to preach and teach not only about the kingdom, but now about His role in ushering that kingdom.

At first they were happy to hear Him because many had seen Him cleanse the temple in Jerusalem and so wanted to hear Him preach in their hometown (John 4:43-45).

32. Another miracle at Cana

John 4:46-54

Jesus returned, probably to the friend or relative where the wedding had been held, for a visit. While there a royal official (one of Herod's household?) comes to Him to heal his son lying sick across the lake at his home in Capernaum. Jesus sends him home telling him his son is well and while on his way the man learns that the child was healed at the point where Jesus said for him to return.

This is the only miracle recorded during this period of His Galilean ministry. It is interesting to note this is the first time that the writers associate faith in Jesus with the miraculous healings. The man and his entire household became disciples after this incident.

This is the end of this section, after this miracle and teaching in the area Jesus will return to Jerusalem for the second Passover in His ministry. The events covered in this chapter took place over a period of approximately one year.

Lessons

1. Jesus was not soft

A lot of images show Jesus as soft, all love and tenderness, forgiving and kind. He is all of these things, but His appearance at the temple showed that He is also a zealous Lord who hates sin, hates unholiness, hates worldliness, hates hypocrisy.

We must not forget that when Jesus returns, He will not do so as a suffering savior, but as the Lord of Lords coming to judge and punish the unfaithful and wicked, and reward those who have been true to Him.

2. Christians must be ready to pay the price

John lived like a hermit, he preached an unpopular message; his job was to prepare the way for the glory of another, not himself; he died as a martyr for his faith. We all pay a certain price to follow Christ (different with each person), however, when we go into the waters of baptism to bury our old man of sin and die with Christ – what we must realize is that we've given up the claim to own or control our physical lives. God may permit us to have it for a while, or He may just require us to give it up for Christ in one day.

When you become a Christian you are either going to give your life to God:

- One day at a time in service, worship, giving, suffering, or
- Give it to Him all at once if He requires you to be martyred.

Either way, it belongs to Him and He will require it of us somehow.

Whether it's one day at a time or all at once, let's be like John: happy and joyful that we must decrease so that Christ can increase.

READING ASSIGNMENT FOR CHAPTER 5

33. John 5:1-47

34. Luke 14:14-30

35. Matthew 4:13-17; Mark 1:21-28; Luke 4:31-37

36. Matthew 8:14-17; Mark 1:29-34; Luke 4:38-41

37. Matthew 4:18-22; Mark 1:16-20; Luke 5:1-11

38. Matthew 4:23-25; Mark 1:35-39; Luke 4:42-44

39. Matthew 8:1-4; Mark 1:40-45; Luke 5:12-16

40. Matthew 9:2-8; Mark 2:1-12; Luke 5:17-26

41. Matthew 9:9-13; Mark 2:13-17; Luke 5:27-32

42. Matthew 9:14-17; Mark 2:18-22; Luke 5:33-39

43. Matthew 12:1-8; Mark 2:23-28; Luke 6:1-5

44. Matthew 12:9-14; Mark 3:1-6; Luke 6:6-11

45. Matthew 12:15-21; Mark 3:7-12

46. Matthew 10:1-42; Mark 3:13-19; Luke 6:12-19

5.
2nd TO 3rd PASSOVER

So far Jesus has spent most of His time in the northern part of the country with only short periods on visits to Jerusalem. After spending the first Passover of His public ministry in Jerusalem, Jesus returns home once again. During the year between the second Passover to the third, the Lord will minister exclusively in the area of Galilee near His original home and the homes of many of His Apostles.

We pick up the story from the point where He was at Cana in the north and returns to Jerusalem for a brief story during the second Passover after which He will turn northward again.

There are thirty-six events recorded during this period. Most are described by Matthew, Mark and Luke with John providing the story of the first incident and sharing a description of the last three.

33. Jesus attends second Passover

John 5:1-47

At His first appearance in the temple, Jesus affected the crowds with His zeal (cleansing the temple) and signs and teaching. The priests saw Him as a nuisance and tried to get rid of Him by confronting Him. This second Passover appearance infuriates the Jews because He does two things:

- He heals a man on the Sabbath and orders him to pick up his pallet and go home. They accused Him of sinning because He had healed (in the Temple of all places) on a Sabbath – this was work. Jesus gave the man instructions to carry his pallet – this was work.

- In His preaching He equates Himself with God: punishable by death if untrue.

His position has gone from challenger and nuisance to enemy and threat. John says that they begin seeking ways to kill Him so that He was now in danger if He stayed in Jerusalem.

34. Return to Galilee

Luke 4:14-30

Luke only begins this section with "and" without connecting it to other events, but the information contained matches other information in Matthew and Mark for this time frame.

Jesus, rejected in Jerusalem, returns to the north once again and goes into His hometown of Nazareth to preach. He also begins to declare His true identity by telling them that a passage in Isaiah concerning the Messiah referred directly to Him personally. His people are amazed since they see Him only as a hometown boy, but when He insists that this is the truth and that if they don't accept it – it will go to the Gentiles (another new development in His preaching). They too become angry and try to mob Him. He escapes their attack and leaves town.

35. Jesus settles in Capernaum

Matthew 4:13-17; Mark 1:21-28; Luke 4:31-37

After His rejection at Nazareth, He goes to His adult home in Capernaum at the north side of the lake and settles there.

Here He teaches and performs a miracle (casts out a demon), but here the people are amazed and spread the knowledge of Him throughout the region, helping the spread of His ministry.

36. Healing of Simon's Mother-in-Law

Matthew 8:14-17; Mark 1:29-34; Luke 4:38-41

These events come close together and are hard to put in order since the writers tell the story differently.

- Preaching and healing at Capernaum
- Healing Simon's Mother-in-Law
- Call to Apostles

However, Mark says that immediately after leaving the synagogue, they went to Peter's house and Jesus healed his Mother-in-Law and many rich who sought Him out. This event leads to the next in logical order.

37. The call of Simon, Andrew, James and John

Matthew 4:18-22; Mark 1:16-20; Luke 5:1-11

Mark is out of sync with his account, but his gospel is a series of snap shots of Jesus' life, not meant to follow a precise chronological order (unlike Luke who is a historian and is more particular).

After the powerful preaching followed by the miracles, even a miracle done for the Apostles themselves (Jesus shows them where to find a huge catch of fish), the Lord takes the opportunity to call 4 men into full-time ministry.

Up until this time these men have continued their work as fishermen and followed Jesus as disciples. But now Jesus calls on them to leave everything to be with Him full-time. Now their training as Apostles will begin in earnest.

38. Circuit preaching through Galilee

Matthew 4:23-25; Mark 1:35-39; Luke 4:42-44

Once Jesus has His disciples called, they set out on a preaching tour of the region. His miracles and teaching, as well as the news of His activity in Jerusalem had caused a great interest in the north. Jesus begins the training process of His newly called Apostles by taking them along on the speaking tour that He had up until this point done largely on His own.

39. Jesus heals a leper

Matthew 8:1-4; Mark 1:40-45; Luke 5:12-16

The Jews believed that when the Messiah came, He would be able to cure lepers. This leper comes to Jesus convinced that Jesus could cure him – and Jesus does. His reason for coming was faith that Jesus was the Messiah.

Jesus tells him not to tell anyone (to avoid people coming for a cure, but not related to faith). The man is overjoyed and can't contain himself and tells everyone. This causes the Lord to avoid the cities because of the crowds searching for Him and looking for a sign or miracle.

40. Return to Capernaum

Matthew 9:2-8; Mark 2:1-12; Luke 5:17-26

The leper's unwanted publicity seems to have forced an end to the preaching tour and Jesus returns to His home in Capernaum. While He is in His home there are crowds that come to hear Him speak – even at His house.

It was during this time that several men, who couldn't get inside the house through the door, decide to remove the tile from His roof and lower one of their paralyzed friends through so he could be with the Lord. Jesus forgives the man's sins first (to show His divine authority) and when the scribes sitting there questioned if He had authority, Jesus healed the man to show that He had both the authority to forgive sins and the power to heal since one goes with the other (only God can heal/only God can forgive) – if you can do one you can do the other.

41. The calling of Matthew

Matthew 9:9-13; Mark 2:13-17; Luke 5:27-32

After this event He was by the Sea of Galilee where He found and called Matthew as His next Apostle.

So far, most of His Apostles are relatives and fishermen from His own region. Matthew is not a relative or fisherman, but a despised tax collector for the region. He collected Roman tax and tacked on a collecting fee for his services. He, as a tax collector for a foreign government, was considered a sinner along with gamblers, thieves, herdsmen, custom officials, etc. As such, they could not act as judges or witnesses against others because of their moral uncertainty.

Jesus, nevertheless, calls this man to follow and he does so immediately. So enthusiastic is he about his call that he invites Jews to his home for a feast. Many of his "sinner" friends are there and this causes the Jews to murmur that Jesus is associating with sinners. Jesus was associating with sinners, but not to share their sins, He was there to call them out of their sins.

42. Questions on fasting

Matthew 9:14-17; Mark 2:18-22; Luke 5:33-39

43. Questions on working

Matthew 12:1-8; Mark 2:23-28; Luke 6:1-5

44. Pharisees plot His death

Matthew 12:9-14; Mark 3:1-6; Luke 6:6-11

Now that He has saturated the north with His healings, miracles, teaching and witnessing about Himself there begins a concerted effort to discredit Him and His teaching – blowback!

At first it was John's disciples along with the Pharisees' disciples who challenged the Apostles because they did not fast. Then it was the Pharisees who challenged them for eating corn they picked on the Sabbath. Of course the answer to these and all other objections was that Jesus was the Messiah and in His presence no fasting was required, and in His service all work was blessed at all times.

Of course the Pharisees rejected the claim of His being the Messiah and when their efforts to discredit Him fail, they began to try to silence Him for good.

45. Jesus withdraws from the attacks

Matthew 12:15-21; Mark 3:7-12

The confrontations and plots to take His life force Him to withdraw from the public places. However, this does not stop the crowds from coming to Him – all the way from Jerusalem. Jesus teaches and heals all who come to Him.

46. Jesus appoints the twelve

Matthew 10:1-42; Mark 3:13-19; Luke 6:12-19

His ministry has grown so large that He cannot easily move from place to place because of the crowds; He cannot venture into the main cities without drawing violence towards Himself.

After a long night of prayer, Jesus chooses among His many disciples, 12 who will become His Apostles.

- Disciples are ones who follow.
- Apostles are messengers who are sent ahead.

These twelve men who have been disciples from the beginning of His ministry are called to be in exclusive service to Him and the gospel as Apostles. He gives them instructions about their work and empowers them for the task.

This will change the nature and growth of His ministry as the Apostles will now begin to bring the message ahead of Jesus in preparation for His coming into a place.

Lessons

Although this section describes much of Jesus' work in the north and the growing opposition towards Him, one thread that's seen through these events is the approach and work of "ministry." For example:

1. Ministry is in stages

Note that God sent Jesus out in stages; as a child, a boy, family, region, main cities, disciples, messengers, etc. Note also that the disciples grew in their time and commitment – first part-time disciples, then Apostles, finally giving their lives to God in death.

In the end God will want us to be with Him and devoted to Him forever (a joy for us) and so as disciples and ministers we are, in this life, working our way towards that total devotion now.

- If you don't want that now, you're not going to have it later.

- Those who love the world (even if they say they are Christians) do so at the expense of devoting themselves to God.

- We need to check which way we're going; more devoted to God or less?

2. Ministry is like stone polishing

The example of what Jesus did with the Apostles is much like what He does with us in the church. He took 12 very different men (zealots, tax collectors, fishermen, intellectuals, etc.) and like 12 uncut, unpolished stones, He put them in a bag and shook them together for three years. Circumstances, work, challenges, etc.

After 3 years 11 of them came out smooth and polished like jewels – and one was crushed to dust (Judas).

It's the same way with us in the church. Jesus takes different people with different backgrounds, puts us all in a bag and shakes us up for a lifetime. Some will come out as smooth and polished stones ready for His crown by faithfully persevering in faith and in love; and some will be turned to dust because of unfaithfulness, sinfulness and lack of commitment.

READING ASSIGNMENT FOR CHAPTER 6

47. Matthew 5:1-8:1; Luke 6:20-49
48. Matthew 8:5-13; Luke 7:1-10
49. Luke 7:11-17
50. Matthew 11:20-30
51. Luke 7:36-50
52. Luke 8:1-3
53. Matthew 12:22-37; Mark 3:22-30; Luke 11:14-15
54. Matthew 12:38-45; Luke 11:16, 24-36
55. Matthew 12:46-50; Mark 3:20-21; 31-35; Luke 8:19-21
56. Matthew 13:1-53; Mark 4:1-34; Luke 8:4-18
57. Matthew 8:18-27; Mark 4:35-41; Luke 8:22-25
58. Matthew 8:28-34; Mark 5:1-20; Luke 8:26-40
59. Matthew 9:1; 18-26; Mark 5:21-43; Luke 8:41-56
60. Matthew 9:27-34
61. Matthew 13:54-58; Mark 6:1-6
62. Matthew 9:35-38; Mark 6:6
63. Matthew 10:1-11:1; Mark 6:7-13; Luke 9:1-6
64. Matthew 14:1-12; Mark 6:14-29; Luke 9:7-9
65. Matthew 14:13-21; Mark 6:30-44; Luke 9:10-17; John 6:1-14
66. Matthew 14:22-23; Mark 6:45-56; John 6:15-21
67. John 6:22-71

6.
2nd TO 3rd PASSOVER CONTINUED

In the last chapter we reviewed the activity of Jesus beginning from the second Passover in His ministry to the third. This would be the second year of His public ministry. We noted that during this time He spent most of His time in the northern part of the country near His hometown and the area where most of His disciples lived.

During this period He became more bold in declaring His identity and we saw His following increase greatly – to the point where He could no longer move about freely. It was during this second year that He officially appointed the twelve as His Apostles.

In this chapter we will continue with the events that finish out that second year of ministry in the area of Galilee.

47. Sermon on the Mount

Matthew 5:1-8:1; Luke 6:20-49

The Sermon on the Mount is probably the most compact teaching covering the Christian experience found in the New Testament. It is also recorded by Luke in a different variation which suggests that this was the heart of Jesus' preaching and He may have repeated this on a number of occasions. (If you have a good sermon, why not preach it more than once?)

The "Beatitudes" as some call them, describe the attitude and spirit of one who had been freed from the Law and was now motivated by grace, enabled by the Holy Spirit and guided by the Word of Christ. How else could the meek be happy; how else could one see God; inherit the earth; rejoice at persecution; etc.

What Jesus describes in this sermon is the life of one who lives in the kingdom, which had not yet come but was about to be established with His death and resurrection. The Sermon on the Mount is a preview of the church and its life.

48. Healing of the Centurion's servant

Matthew 8:5-13; Luke 7:1-10

This miracle took place in Capernaum, Jesus' adult hometown. What was interesting in His dialogue with this man was that Jesus has just preached a sermon about the kingdom and life in the kingdom to the Jews (who assumed that it was all for them because they were Jews). In healing this non-Jew's servant, Jesus reminds His hearers that entry into the kingdom is based on faith, not culture or tradition. The Centurion believed Jesus and the Jews were amazed at his faith, which Jesus had not yet seen among the Jews.

This is what made the people angry with Him. The leaders were upset with Him because He threatened their authority; the people were upset because He offered the kingdom to both Jews and Gentiles based on faith – no special treatment for the Jews except receiving the first invitation.

49. Raising the widow's son

Luke 7:11-17

This is one of the three times Jesus performs the miracle of raising someone from the dead (Jairus' daughter and Lazarus).

Aside from being a mighty sign in itself, it was also a proof that He was the Messiah since the Scriptures said the Messiah would be able to do this. It was also a preview of His own resurrection. One who had the power to raise others from the grave (not once, but 3 times) could also be raised from the dead Himself.

50. Jesus rebukes the unbelieving cities

Matthew 11:20-30

Even though there was interest and crowds, even though He performs many miracles and teaches for a long period of time – the main cities in the area (Capernaum, Bethsaida, Chorazin) all fail to accept Him or recognize Him as Messiah.

Jesus does two things in response to their rejection:

- He rebukes them and warns them of their eventual judgment and destruction.
- He invites those who are burdened and weakened to come to Him.

The point is that these cities felt themselves to be too wise and superior to believe in Him, so He rejects them and invites the lowly to come.

51. Woman anoints Jesus' feet

Luke 7:36-50

Jesus is eating with Simon the Pharisee. While eating, a woman comes and anoints his feet with her tears and perfume and kisses them and dries them with her hair.

It is ironic that Simon personifies all the cities that Jesus rebuked earlier with his self-righteous attitude towards the woman (he rejects her because she is a sinner), and his unbelieving attitude towards Jesus (did not honor Him in any way by washing His feet or anointing Him with oil).

The woman, on the other hand, represents all those weary and heavy laden people Jesus called to Himself. She brought her sorrow and tears and guilt and laid them at Jesus' feet and left unburdened and forgiven.

There is another time when Jesus has His feet washed, but it will be by Mary (the sister of Martha) and near the end of Jesus' ministry.

52. More circuit preaching in Galilee

Luke 8:1-3

Jesus continues His preaching ministry with the Apostles. This time Luke mentions how His ministry was financed: many of the wealthy women from the king's court helped support Jesus and the Apostles in their ministry.

53. Jesus heals a demoniac

Matthew 12:22-37; Mark 3:22-30; Luke 11:14-15

The significant thing about the healing of this demon-possessed man was that it marked a new line of attack taken against Him by the Pharisees. Obviously the Pharisees, some all the way from Jerusalem, were beginning to target Him more ferociously than before. In the past they tried to discredit His teaching or His authority, now they make an attack against His character saying that He is of the devil (Beelzebub).

Of course Jesus answers that if this is so, then Satan is destroying Himself because He has just cast the devil out of a man, not put him in.

54. The crowd seeks a sign

Matthew 12:38-45; Luke 11:16; 24-36

The Pharisees and Scribes respond by saying that they want a miracle and sign in order to prove Jesus' divinity. He tells them that aside from the ones already done, the one true sign that will settle the matter will be His death and resurrection. The sign of Jonah is a cryptic way of saying this. The prophets said (David, Acts 2:25-30) that the Messiah would have power over death.

Even Paul in Romans 1:4 says that the resurrection is the definitive proof that Jesus was the Son of God, the Messiah.

55. Jesus' family come for Him

Matthew 12:46-50; Mark 3:20-21; 31-35; Luke 8:19-21

All these accusations, all this confusion, leads His family to come and try to bring Him home thinking He's lost it. Their concern may have been sincere and normal, but it also showed disbelief and Jesus points this out when He claims that those who believe are His true brothers and sisters.

It's the same with us – our true family is our Christian family. If we prefer non-believers (even if they are family) to believers, then we love this world more than the kingdom.

56. Seven parables from a boat

Matthew 13:1-53; Mark 4:1-34; Luke 8:4-18

Again, He is in the Galilee region at Capernaum, his home, and He enters a boat to teach the crowd on shore. The writers record a series of 7 parables strung together as a lesson:

1. The sower and the seed
2. Wheat and tares
3. Mustard seed
4. Leaven
5. Treasure in a field
6. Pearl of great price
7. Dragnet

57. Jesus calms the storm

Matthew 8:18-27; Mark 4:35-41; Luke 8:22-25

58. Jesus cures two demoniacs

Matthew 8:28-34; Mark 5:1-20; Luke 8:26-40

59. Jesus raises Jairus' daughter and cures the woman with hemorrhage

Matthew 9:1; 18-26; Mark 5:21-43; Luke 8:41-56

60. Jesus heals the blind and another demoniac

Matthew 9:27-34

After the long teaching section, the writers describe a series of amazing miracles as Jesus leaves one shore of the lake and crosses over to the other.

On His first pass He miraculously calms a fierce storm. On His arrival He cures a demoniac and sends him off to his native country where Jesus will later go and have great success in preaching. He crosses the lake again and this time raises a young girl from the dead and heals a woman who suffered from an incurable hemorrhage. Finally He cures a blind man and one who was unable to speak.

The net result was that He had performed miracles the like of which had never been done by anyone before. He demonstrated that He had power over the creation, over death, over every kind of disease – exactly the kind of power that no ordinary faith healer could and did have. But only the kind of power God Himself could have.

61. Jesus rejected in Nazareth

Matthew 13:54-58; Mark 6:1-6

Despite all of these signs and wonders, despite all the teaching, His native city still refuses to believe in Him. Despite all of this He visits and tries to reach them.

They don't try to stone Him, but simply refuse to accept Him and for this reason He does no miracles among them.

62. Final preaching tour through Galilee

Matthew 9:35-38; Mark 6:6

Jesus makes one final tour through His native region before going further north and then down to Jerusalem for the feast. He continues to preach, teach and heal where they receive Him (not in His hometown).

63. Jesus sends out the twelve

Matthew 10:1-11:1; Mark 6:7-13; Luke 9:1-6

After several tours with Him, Jesus now sends the twelve out by themselves to begin their public ministry in their own towns and villages.

The writers provide the instructions for ministry that Jesus provided them with and also describe the power He gave them to do their work. They go off with the power to do miracles in His name, power given to confirm their message about the kingdom.

64. Herod takes note of Jesus

Matthew 14:13-21; Mark 6:30-44; Luke 9:10-17; John 6:1-14

All the writers describe the excitement when the Apostles return from their first preaching tour.

He takes them to a quiet place for them to rest after their work. Probably to teach them some more and respond to various questions and problems they may have had. Their success however cuts this short as the crowds find them for more ministry. Jesus responds by teaching them and when the hour is late He performs a great miracle in feeding them (5000) from just a few loaves of bread and fish.

Jesus will perform this miracle again later for 4000 people at another site.

This miracle is a sign of several things:

- Jesus' power over the physical universe and laws.

- A preview of the great spiritual banquet He is preparing in the kingdom.

- An encouragement to rely on Jesus to provide for not only spiritual, but our physical needs as well.

65. The twelve return

Matthew 14:13-21; Mark 6:30-44; Luke 9:10-17; John 6:1-14

66. Jesus sends the twelve across the lake

Matthew 14:22-23; Mark 6:45-56; John 6:15-21

After this "debriefing" and the miracle, Jesus will send them once again across the lake in order to continue their work. It is at this occasion that Jesus came to them while walking upon the water and Peter requested that he too come to Him.

Note that they had themselves performed miracles and so Peter was primed to push the edge of this newly given power by asking to do yet another miraculous thing.

He learned that all is possible, but only through faith, and he learned that his faith still had boundaries.

67. The crowds seek for a sign

John 6:22-71

The people have witnessed many miracles and now find Jesus with the Apostles on the other side of the lake and demand another sign.

They had been fed miraculously the day before and they want more. They would follow a Messiah who provided for not only their spiritual needs, but also their physical needs as well – without any effort by them.

This is the passage where Jesus uses the imagery of bread to describe Himself as the bread from heaven. He also alludes to the communion which He will institute in the future (drink my blood and eat my flesh). The first time He makes the astonishing promise that if someone believes in Him, He will resurrect that person from the dead. This dialogue occurred in the synagogue at Capernaum and because of His teachings (about Him being the bread/manna from heaven; about eating His flesh, etc/ about resurrection) many of the disciples abandoned Him at this point.

It was a critical moment for the Apostles because they had seen and heard so much, now Jesus was speaking of things that they could not comprehend. He challenged their faith and Peter responded (for all the Apostles) that they had no place to go but to Him – despite their lack of understanding – they believed. That is often the case in our lives as well, things happen, we are faced with issues we don't understand – our test is, "do we continue to believe and obey, even though we might not understand why?" – that is what we call walking by faith. Despite the miracles they saw, the teachings they received, even the Apostles had to do a stretch by faith and not by sight.

READING ASSIGNMENT FOR CHAPTER 7

68. Matthew 14:34-36; Mark 6:55-56

69. Matthew 15:1-20; Mark 7:1-23

70. Matthew 15:21-28; Mark 7:24-30

71. Matthew 15:29-38; Mark 7:31-8:9

72. Matthew 15:39-16:4; Mark 8:10-12

73. Matthew 16:5-12; Mark 8:13-21

74. Mark 8:22-26

75. Matthew 16:13-20; Mark 8:27-30; Luke 9:18-21

76. Matthew 16:21-28; Mark 8:31-9:1; Luke 9:22-27

77. Matthew 17:1-13; Mark 9:2-13; Luke 9:28-36

78. Matthew 17:14-21; Mark 9:14-29; Luke 9:37-43

79. Matthew 17:22-23; Mark 9:30-32; Luke 9:44-45

80. Matthew 17:24-27

81. Matthew 18:1-35; Mark 9:33-50; Luke 9:46-50

7.
3rd TO 4th PASSOVER

In the last chapter we finished the events recorded during Jesus' second year of ministry. During this time we see that He is immensely popular, but has made some deadly enemies: the Pharisees and religious leaders want to kill Him, even some of the disciples are leaving because of the demands of His teaching.

Most of His teaching and signs have been performed in the northern part of the country with occasional visits to Jerusalem during key festivals. The Apostles have now been chosen and are ministering on their own in the northern area as well.

As He enters the third year of His ministry He will make more appearances in and around Jerusalem to declare His person and purpose for coming.

We begin the next section of events describing His ministry from the 3rd Passover to the beginning of the Last Passover week.

68. Healings in the Gennesaret area

Matthew 14:34-36; Mark 6:55-56

Our last event found Jesus in the synagogue at Capernaum. Gennesaret was south of Capernaum. Mark says that many were healed simply by touching the "fringe" of His cloak. Like other male Jews, faithful to the Law, He had a blue tassel at each corner of His garment and this is what they reached for in faith.

69. Pharisees question hand washing

Matthew 15:1-20; Mark 7:1-23

Jesus' successful ministry in Gennesaret was interrupted by Pharisees who had come from Jerusalem to observe and confront Him in order to discredit Him. One of their accusations was that His disciples violated the "tradition of the elders" by not observing the ritualistic washing of their hands before eating.

Tradition of the elders referred to a body of rules and regulations created by the scribes that dictated how the Law was to be applied. For example, the Law forbade work on the Sabbath. The scribes created over one hundred definitions of what was considered "work" and "leisure" in order to guide the Jews in keeping that command.

Jesus replied that these things were no more than man made rules that had no authority from God and thus no authority over man. Jesus went on to show that it wasn't dirty hands or even food that defiled a person's soul, it was what came out of the heart that defiled a human's soul. This infuriated the Pharisees because He not only discredited their source of authority (tradition of elders), but also waved away food restrictions to which the Jews held so dearly.

Restricting types of food was a way of distinguishing the people as separate from other nations and a mark of God's chosen people. From now on however, their faith in Christ would do this for them.

70. Jesus heads further north

Matthew 15:21-28; Mark 7:24-30

This break with Jewish tradition was sure to cause even more hatred among Jewish religious leaders so Jesus heads further north into Gentile territory. Here He meets a Syrophoenician woman who is a Gentile and who asks Him to heal her daughter.

Jesus, using the expressions of that day, tells her that He has come to feed the children and not their pets. This is what many Jews thought in those days concerning Gentiles with which they were friendly. The woman recognizing the analogy, and without diminishing the role and privilege of the Jews, says that even the pets get a little of the leftovers after the children have eaten. She would gladly accept that.

In this woman Jesus finds not only a woman of faith, but also a woman of humility, perseverance and courage. He rewards all of this by healing her child without even seeing her.

71. Jesus ministers in Decapolis

Matthew 15:29-38; Mark 7:31-8:9

Decapolis is on the east side of the Sea of Galilee where Jesus healed the demoniac and sent him to spread the news of his cure among the region (10 cities).

Jesus now returns and heals a man who is deaf and a great multitude is assembled to hear Him preach. This is the result of the work of this demoniac. Jesus not only teaches them, but also performs the miracle of the multiplication of bread and fish for this group – a miracle He has done for the second time.

72. Jesus confronted again by Pharisees

Matthew 15:39-16:4; Mark 8:10-12

Jesus finishes in the area of the Decapolis and crosses the Sea of Galilee. Once there the Pharisees are ready with another attack, this time to challenge Him by asking for a sign from "heaven." Their point was that His miracles were not spectacular enough. They wanted an Old Testament miracle where the sun stood still or fire and brimstone were called down from the sky.

Jesus rebukes them for their blindness in that they can tell what the weather is from the color of the sky, but can't even interpret all of the signs He has already done to prove His legitimacy.

He refuses to give them such a sign and refers them to the story of Jonah and tells them that this will be the definitive sign that He is from God.

- Jonah 3 days in the whale and survived.
- Jesus 3 days in the tomb and resurrected.

The resurrection will be the sign for everyone, including them, that He is the Messiah sent from God.

73. Discussion with Apostles in the boat

Matthew 16:5-12; Mark 8:13-21

The Apostles had been travelling with Jesus through all these events. They had seen the confrontations with the Pharisees, the miracles, the feeding of the 4,000. Now they were once again crossing the Sea of Galilee and Jesus tries to warn them concerning the Pharisees and their hypocrisy. The reason for this is that the Apostles will also have to deal with these people in their ministry.

Jesus uses a figure of speech that they don't understand – "leaven of the Pharisees" – and explains that the Pharisees' false ideas introduced as doctrine from God had taken such a hold that the people accepted it as Law.

The Apostles think He's scolding them because they forgot to bring the leftover bread from the feeding. This shows how unsophisticated and hard hearted they were and certainly no match for the Pharisees

74. Jesus heals a blind man

Mark 8:22-26

Upon arriving on the other side, the people bring Him a blind man to cure and Jesus does so in stages, putting first saliva on his eyes then laying hands on them. This was probably done to help his faith develop in stages as well. First saliva to know that Jesus was doing something for him, then complete healing once he realized that it was Jesus who was giving him sight.

75. Peter's confession

Matthew 16:13-20; Mark 8:27-30; Luke 9:18-21

Jesus had been challenged by the Pharisees and debated with them. He was still training and preparing His Apostles to carry on their ministry. After all that had happened He tested to see if they remained convinced of His identity. Without this certainty they would not be able to withstand what was to come in Jerusalem in the not too distant future.

Jesus asks them of their assessment of Him, and Peter answers for the group in confessing Jesus as the Christ, the Messiah sent from God.

Now Jesus wants them to be assured of this, but He is not prepared for them to confess this yet; this will come after His death and resurrection.

76. Jesus foretells His death and resurrection

Matthew 16:21-28; Mark 8:31-9:1; Luke 9:22-27

Now that they have expressed their belief in His true identity, Jesus can further teach them on the purpose of His ministry – to die and resurrect according to the Word. This is the first time He tells them this and they are in shock. So much so that Peter, once again, tried to talk Jesus out of doing this. He is trying to protect his vision of what the Messiah should or shouldn't do and guarding his own place as an Apostle – no good being the Apostle of a dead Messiah. Jesus rebukes him sharply for his very human and selfish motives.

77. The transfiguration

Matthew 17:1-13; Mark 9:2-13; Luke 9:28-36

After the first prophecy of His death He takes Peter, James and John up on a mountain and is transfigured into His glorious state. Luke says He discusses His coming death with Moses and Elijah. Again Peter responds foolishly by wanting to make (booths) tents that will house all of them so they can stay on the mountain in this state. God speaks saying, "This is my beloved Son, in whom I am well pleased, listen to Him." The point here is that Moses represents the Law, Elijah the Prophets. Now God wants the people to listen to Jesus – He fulfills the Law and Prophets.

78. Casting out a demon that the Apostles could not

Matthew 17:14-21; Mark 9:14-29; Luke 9:37-43

When they returned to join the other Apostles, they were embroiled in an argument with the Scribes over a healing they were unable to do. Jesus casts a demon out of a boy and rebukes the Apostles for their lack of faith and prayer. They had power to do this in the past, but had perhaps forgotten that every miracle and healing was based on faith in God and they were taking more credit than they needed to. The argument with he Scribes suggests that they may have wanted to impress them.

79. Jesus foretells His death and resurrection a second time

Matthew 17:22-23; Mark 9:30-32; Luke 9:44-45

Between the first and second times Jesus foretells of His impending death, there are tremendous miracles and signs that take place – still in the northern region, but further north and west.

After He casts out the demon, Jesus mentions again that He will eventually be killed, but this time adds the idea that He will be betrayed. They ask no more questions of Him because they do not like the answers He's giving them, they are in denial.

80. Money from a fish

Matthew 17:24-27

Each male 20 and over had to pay a temple tax. Not to do so was an act of Apostasy. Jesus claimed exemption because as the Son of the Father whose house was the Temple, He should not have to pay. But to not cause stumbling He miraculously makes a coin appear in the mouth of a fish that Peter catches in order to pay for Himself and Peter.

Some speculate that since Jesus only paid for Himself and Peter the other Apostles were under 20 at the time. This makes sense, the average age at the time was around 50. Peter was old when he died in 63-64; John was very old 100 AD (80-90).

81. Who is the greatest

Matthew 18:1-35; Mark 9:33-50; Luke 9:46-50

A dispute arises among them as to who will be the greatest among them in the kingdom. They are still very much under the impression that the kingdom will be some earthly form of government.

Jesus responds to this with a variety of teachings:

- The childlike attitude needed to enter and stay in the kingdom.
- The danger of making a child of God lose their faith, or leading one into sin.
- A discourse on how to deal with disputes among brethren (go alone, bring another, tell the church, etc.).
- A parable about the necessity of forgiveness (the hard-hearted slave who refused to forgive).

All of these teachings are to try to make them understand that relationships in the kingdom are not based on being great through power and control, but being great based on love, mercy and service.

Mark adds that they also wanted to condemn others who were working in Jesus' name but not part of their group, and Jesus restrained them saying that if you're with Jesus you're with His followers as well.

With this Jesus' northern ministry will be coming to a close. He will make more trips south until the last week of His life that He will spend in the city where He will be rejected, condemned and crucified.

Lessons

1. Understanding comes after faith

Note that every time the Apostles expressed their faith in progressive degrees – following Jesus, staying with Him when others rejected, actually acknowledging Him as Messiah – Jesus rewarded them with a clearer vision of who He was. Each time they obeyed and walked by faith He rewarded that faith with a great miracle, a vision, a confirmation that their faith was valid.

It's the same with us today. We don't get understanding and then we believe – it works the other way around. I believe, I obey, then I grow in my understanding and reassurance that what I believed was true. I'm more sure now of God's forgiveness and promise of the Holy Spirit than I was the day I believed and was baptized. He has rewarded my original faith.

2. Unity to the head = unity to the body

The Apostles didn't want anyone claiming Jesus unless they were part of their group. Jesus said if you're united to Me, you're united to the body. It also works in reverse, if you're not united to the body, you're not united to the head.

Jesus died for the church, His body, and union with Him automatically means union with the church. You can't separate the two.

READING ASSIGNMENT FOR CHAPTER 8

82. John 7:1-53

83. John 8:1-11

84. John 8:12-59

85. John 9:1-41

86. John 10:1-21

87. Luke 9:51-62

88. Luke 10:1-24

89. Luke 10:25-37

90. Luke 10:38-11:13

91. Luke 11:14-54

92. Luke 12:1-13:5

93. Luke 13:6-9

94. Luke 13:10-17

8.
3rd TO 4th PASSOVER
CONTINUED

We were describing events that took place between the 3rd and the beginning of the 4th Passover in Jesus' public ministry. During this final phase Jesus was spending more time in and around Jerusalem, going into the city to teach and then returning north when the situation became too dangerous.

We pick up the story as the Lord is teaching in the northern part of the country. Important feasts are fast approaching and He will leave the relative safety of His home area and venture into Jerusalem once more in order to teach and declare His true nature and mission to the people in the holy city.

Event number 82 describes one such dynamic appearance in Jerusalem during the feast of Tabernacles (Booths).

82. Jesus at Jerusalem during Feast of Tabernacles

John 7:1-53

The Feast of Tabernacles was a celebration that commemorated several things: the blessings of harvest as well as the time spent in the desert during the Exodus. Features of this feast:

- The name booths/tabernacles comes from the booths made of tree boughs and branches they all had to live in during the 7 days of the feast.

- It was one of the 3 annual feasts that every male had to attend.

- It came at the end of fall and was a time of celebrating.

- Jews today still celebrate this feast by building "booths" in yards and porches.

During this time Jesus is in Galilee and his brothers taunt Him to come to the feast to prove Himself, if He really is the Messiah. He refuses to be provoked by them but does secretly go to the feast.

While there He observes that the people have a divided opinion about Him (He's evil and an imposter / He's a good man). To clarify their opinion, He stands up publicly and begins to teach the crowds on several occasions. This is the time where He:

- Accuses them of trying to kill Him, the one who has brought the teaching of God.

- He says that He is sent directly from God.

- "Where I am you cannot come."

- "Let Him come to Me and drink."

All of His references are to declare that He is from God and equal to God, and for this reason the religious leaders send soldiers to arrest Him but they don't carry out their mission because of His teaching. When the soldiers come back empty handed there is a dispute among the leaders at which time Nicodemus tries to defend Jesus but is put down by the other leaders.

83. Jesus and the adulteress

John 8:1-11

The Lord leaves the temple area and goes to the Mount of Olives. There is a park there (Gethsemane) where He will later pray before His arrest. He spends the night here and returns to the temple the next day.

The Pharisees try a new line of attack, this time trying to turn the people against Him. They do this by bringing a woman caught in an adulteress affair and asking Him what to do with her. If, according to Mosaic law, He tells them that she should be stoned, they will accuse Him of being unmerciful and even breaking Roman law because Jews weren't allowed to execute without Roman permission. If He tells them to let her go, they will accuse Him of being too liberal and turn the people against Him.

Jesus turns the tables on the Pharisees by challenging them to consider who among them was truly worthy of being this woman's judge: "Let he who is without sin cast the first stone."

When they realize that according to Law and conscience, none of them are worthy to judge her, they leave. Then Jesus, who is worthy to judge her, does so by forgiving her and encouraging her to not sin in this way any longer.

To the crowd He proves His unassailable wisdom. To the woman He demonstrates the mercy of God.

84. Jesus teaches again in the temple

John 8:12-59

Once the meeting with the woman is over, Jesus again begins to teach the crowds concerning His identity and responds to their questions and attacks.

- I am the light of the world
- Where I am going you cannot come
- When you lift up the Son of Man, you will know that I am He
- If you abide in my word, you are truly disciples of mine
- You are of your father the devil
- Before Abraham was, I am

These and other teachings concerning His true identity as the divine Son of God and Messiah provoked them to such frenzy that they took up stones and tried to kill Him on the spot, but He escaped.

85. Jesus heals the blind beggar

John 9:1-41

Jesus has left the temple area for safety's sake, but continues to minister in the area. The Lord heals a man blind from birth and when this fact is presented to the Jewish leaders they accept that the miracle is genuine, but continue to reject Jesus. This was significant for two reasons:

1. The healing of a blind person was never done before and was a definitive sign that Jesus was the Messiah and they rejected this clear demonstration.

2. The healing was a living parable that pointed to their own blindness in the spiritual world and how God was opening the eyes of the simple and shutting the eyes of the proud.

This sign was a judgment directly on Jewish leaders and teachers who should have seen, but didn't.

86. Jesus' discourse on the good shepherd

John 10:1-21

Jesus' final teaching in the temple area before returning north after the feast was about the Good Shepherd. He has plainly declared who He was and that His time was at hand. He is forcing the people to choose who they will follow. He declares that He is the Good Shepherd and those who follow Him are following the right leader. This was a rebuke to the Jewish leaders that were leading at that time.

It is interesting to note that after this final speech and invitation to follow Him, there was still a division over Him: some believed He was possessed, others who knew about the healing of the blind man were impressed. Yet with all of His teaching and the great miracle, there was still doubt and division among the people.

87. Final departure from Galilee to Jerusalem

Luke 9:51-62

There is no transitional explanation of Jesus' leaving Jerusalem and going back up north. The next scene finds Him back in Galilee between the fall feast of Booths and the winter feast of Dedication.

At this point we see Him preparing for yet another trip to Jerusalem to teach at the temple. Things have cooled down and He is planning to return. During this trip there are some who want to go with Him and it is here that He warns them about the cost of discipleship after one follower wants to go to his father's funeral before going with Jesus.

Discipleship is serious business and Jesus warns that those who, "...put their hand to the plow and look back are not fit for the kingdom of God."

88. Jesus sends the seventy

Luke 10:1-24

After the warning to those who would be disciples, Jesus chooses seventy of His present followers and empowers them to preach and minister to the people. They return reporting that their special gifts were effective in healing and casting out demons. Jesus reminds them that their true joy and security lie in the fact that they themselves are in the book of life (saved). We now have the Apostles and 70 special disciples who are preaching and ministering in the area causing quite a stir and preparing for Jesus' final entry into Jerusalem.

89. The parable of the Good Samaritan

Luke 10:25-37

During this time Jesus presents a parable in response to a question from a scribe who wanted to justify himself in regards to keeping the Law. The scribe thought that the important provisions in the Law concerning love and obedience pertained only to the Jews.

Jesus teaches them the parable of the Good Samaritan in order to show that God's Law is universal and applies to all. Everyone will be judged by God based on their obedience to Him and their treatment of others. He reminds them that before God, all are neighbors and worthy of love.

90. Jesus visits Mary and Martha in Bethany

Luke 10:38-11:13

This was Jesus' place to stay when going to teach in Jerusalem since it was only a few miles from the city. During this occasion Martha asks Jesus to get Mary to help with the serving. Jesus shows that being with Him is the best choice and He won't push people away who prefer this. At the same time the disciples ask Him to help them pray and Jesus teaches them using another version of the Lord's Prayer also recorded in Matthew 6:9.

91. Jesus cures another demoniac

Luke 11:14-54

In this passage the cure is hardly mentioned at all. Luke describes in detail the reaction of the people and the Pharisees who witnessed this miracle. Some accused Jesus of using Satan's power to do miracles and healings, others wanted more signs. The Pharisees continued to attack Him on points of ceremony and tradition (IE-washing of hands).

As Jesus' ministry neared its end, His miracles provoked confusion among the doubters and anger among His enemies. Jesus responded by rebuking them and warning them that they risked condemnation and punishment because of their disbelief.

92. Exhortation to His disciples

Luke 12:1-13:5

Jesus is being attacked and opposed by the leaders. The people are unsure of Him. He encourages and comforts His disciples during this difficult period:

- Be careful of the Pharisees.
- The truth will come out one day (no confusion).
- Fear God, not man.
- God loves you and will care for you (sparrow).
- God will provide what to say and how to respond during persecution.

Jesus is beginning to prepare His disciples for His death and resurrection and the difficult times ahead. He tells them the parable of the Rich Fool (bigger barns) in order to warn them not to get too tied up in this world. Much of His exhortation is similar to early teachings given to them in the Sermon on the Mount.

Jesus also adds new parables during this time as well: slaves who are faithful when their master comes and do not let their house be broken into; slaves that act faithfully and honorably while their master is away.

He finishes His teachings to His disciples and to the people who had gathered to hear Him. He knows that His cross and resurrection are near and wants to warn them that an important time of decision is near.

93. Parable of the Barren Fig Tree

Luke 13:6-9

Jesus provides one more parable that warns disciples of the consequences of not producing fruit. The fig tree in the parable was given extra time to produce but would be cut down if it did not eventually produce figs. In all of the teachings and parables at this point, Jesus is issuing a warning to those who have thus far rejected Him.

94. Healing of a woman with a spirit of infirmity

Luke 13:10-17

Jesus is still in the general area of Jerusalem teaching in a local synagogue. Once again He is faced with the challenge of healing on the Sabbath, but does so and rebukes those who would accuse Him of sin for helping a poor woman out of her misery. Luke says that the leaders were humiliated by His rebuke but the people rejoiced at His answer.

In the next chapter we'll continue this section as Jesus will once again go to the Temple to confront the leaders during the Feast of Dedication.

Lessons

1. Time does run out

The Jews had 1500 years to prepare. It seemed that their time would never end, but one day their time did run out. God sent prophets and eventually sent Jesus to prepare them and warn them, but they didn't listen and were destroyed as a nation in 70 AD when the Roman army destroyed the city and killed most of its inhabitants.

Jesus sent His Apostles and in every generation sends His preachers to tell people to be ready. It seems like the Lord will never come, but one day time will run out.

2. The time to do good is now

Whenever the opportunity and the will of God were present, Jesus did good and healed the people. He did this even when it was inconvenient, dangerous or unpopular. The opportunity to do good, to serve or to do right is not always convenient or easy but we must seize it when we can.

Don't talk yourself out of doing good or doing the right thing – you'll lose a blessing if you do.

READING ASSIGNMENT FOR CHAPTER 9

95. John 10:22-42

96. Luke 13:22; John 11:1-16

97. Luke 13:31-35

98. Luke 14:1-6

99. Luke 14:7-24

100. Luke 14:25-35

101. Luke 15:1-32

102. Luke 16:1-31

103. Luke 17:1-10

104. John 11:17-46

105. John 11:47-53

106. John 11:54

9.
3rd TO LAST PASSOVER

We continue with our work on the section of Jesus' ministry that spans from the 3rd Passover to the beginning of the last Passover week. During this period Jesus will spend much time in and around Jerusalem teaching and dealing with the Jewish religious leaders. In the end, they will reject and threaten Him and He will once again retreat to the northern territory before He makes His final entry to Jerusalem to suffer and die and then be resurrected.

95. Jesus at the Feast of Dedication

John 10:22-42

The Feast of Dedication/Lights/Hanukkah was a feast lasting eight days commemorating the time when the temple was rededicated after being desecrated by a foreign king.

Antiochus IV, a Greek ruler, forbade Jewish worship and tried to bring Greek influence into Jewish life. He brought unclean things and animals into the temple (IE-sacrificed a pig on the altar). The Jews revolted (Maccabean Revolt 200 BC) and regained their freedom and set about to reinstate public worship and rededicate the temple. It was during this time of religious renewal that the party of the Pharisees (separated ones) rose up to champion the purity of Jewish life and Scripture in rejecting foreign influences (Greek). The Pharisees were heroes among the people at first.

When the temple was rededicated, the lamp (oil lamp) in the temple was relit, but there was only enough oil for one night.

According to Jewish writings (Talmud), not Scripture, the lamp burned for eight days with only one day's worth of oil. This event was commemorated with the Feast of Lights.

The modern celebration uses a Menorah(type of candlestick) that has seven lights. The middle or top light is called the "Shamash" or "Sentry." It is lit first to provide a useful light in order to see. The other six lights are not to be lit for utilitarian purposes. Their purpose is for a witness and remembrance of the festival. In the same way, Christians don't eat unleavened bread as food – we use it as an emblem of Christ's body when we take communion. The Jews light one of the six lights each night during the festival.

It is during this occasion that Jesus declares His Oneness with God and the Jews try to kill him (3rd time). He appeals to them to believe based on His works alone, but they refuse and try to seize Him. He escapes to Peraea near the Jordan River where He had worked with John and those who were there believed in Him.

96. Journey to Bethany to minister to Lazarus

Luke 13:22; John 11:1-16

During His preaching Jesus receives word that His friend, Lazarus, is deathly ill and that He is needed. Jesus purposely remains where He is for several more days before returning to Bethany to care for Lazarus.

The Apostles are afraid and confused. Jesus refers to Lazarus as "asleep" so they question why they should go to Bethany in the first place. Jesus has to tell them in plain words that he is dead. At this point the Apostles don't understand why Jesus still wants to go. They are also afraid to go near Jerusalem (Bethany where Lazarus lived was only

2-3 miles from Jerusalem). Jesus has narrowly escaped death so they don't want to go back.

Thomas breaks the deadlock by declaring that he's ready to die following the Lord so they are encouraged and agree to follow Jesus back to Bethany.

97. Another threat from Herod

Luke 13:31-35

While this was going on, Jesus receives other news that would normally prevent Him from going into crowded or public places where He was known. The Pharisees approach Him with the message that Herod is out to kill Him. Jesus responds that although cunning, Herod cannot hurt Him before His time and ministry are over.

It is at this point that Jesus laments over Jerusalem, knowing that the people were going to reject Him. There would be more miracles and teaching, but Jesus knew and declared at this point the final outcome of the Jewish reaction concerning Him: rejection and death; and God's reaction concerning them: rejection and judgment.

98. Cure of the man with dropsy

Luke 14:1-6

Between the time of the news about Lazarus and His eventual arrival at Bethany, Jesus spends several days continuing to minister and heal. One of these healings is of the man with dropsy who came to Him (or was put there to test Him by the Pharisees).

Apparently He was having a meal with Pharisees and others when this person suffering from dropsy (not a disease but a symptom of heart, kidney or liver disease), usually a swelling of the body due to water retention. The Pharisees were waiting to see if Jesus would heal this man on the Sabbath. They knew He could heal him, they just wanted to see if He'd do it in such a way as to accuse Him of something.

Jesus asks them if they would save one of their animals on the Sabbath and if so why condemn Him for saving a human being. After this He went ahead and cured this person. They had no reply.

99. Parable of the Great Supper

Luke 14:7-24

After the healing Jesus gives them a parable concerning the guests that were at the meal and teaches them several lessons with it:

- Don't take the best seat until invited so you won't be embarrassed. The principle of the kingdom is that those who raise themselves up will be humbled and those who humble themselves will be honored.

- Don't do good to get a reward or a favor returned. Do good to help those in need regardless of what they can do for you. Your reward for good is always from God, no matter what the world does or does not do.

- Those who refuse God's invitation to be with Him will be left out and others will take their place at the heavenly banquet.

This parable was meant for these Pharisees who refused God's invitation to the heavenly banquet through Christ, thinking they would get there without Him.

Once again Jesus warns them that one way or another God will be glorified, if the Jews didn't do it, He would receive glory by honoring the Gentiles.

100. The cost of discipleship

Luke 14:25-35

After leaving the banquet Jesus continues to teach the crowds that follow Him. He teaches them more deeply on the meaning of discipleship. He shows them that it is more than just following Him around to witness miracles and listen to His teachings. Discipleship requires several things:

- An absolute devotion to the Lord beyond that of family, even one's own life. Anyone or thing that becomes an obstacle to following the Lord needs to be overcome. It doesn't necessarily have to be a sin. If it comes between you and Jesus, it needs to go.

- A willingness to suffer for the Lord and one's faith is a necessary component to being a disciple.

- An understanding that discipleship will require these things and a readiness to go ahead anyways.

- A desire to live life in such a way (IE-salt) as to make a difference in this world and not be conformed to this world.

Jesus regularly pruned His disciples with these teachings to cut away those who were just curious, who didn't really believe or who loved sin more than they loved God. In many ways He still does this today by forcing us to choose Christian living over sinful living; the Bible way over man's way; church life over worldly life; quality over quantity; purity over popularity; devoted over dynamic.

101. Parables of lost people and things

Luke 15:1-32

Once the banquet is over Jesus moves about the general populace and is crowded by publicans and sinners who also wanted to hear Him teach and preach. The Pharisees and Scribes grumbled about this accusing Jesus of associating and eating with undesirables. His response to their criticism was to tell the crowd several parables: the lost sheep, the lost coin and the lost son.

The point of all of these was twofold: God searches for those that are lost, even if it's only one; God rejoices when the lost are found, no matter how lost they were.

The Pharisees and Jews in general had forgotten that God's mission and their purpose was to save lost man. They thought God simply chose them as His people and rejected the rest.

Jesus reminded the sinners that there was hope for them and rebuked the Jews for having neglected their original mission – to be a light unto the Gentiles and prepare the way for the coming of the Savior of the entire world, not just the Jews.

102. Parables of the unjust steward and rich man and Lazarus

Luke 16:1-31

The parables spoken to the crowds were followed by two parables shared only with His disciples. This was probably done as they travelled along on their way to Bethany and Lazarus who awaited.

A. Unjust Steward

This parable focuses on a disciple's need to serve only God and do so sincerely. Jesus makes several points including the ideas that if one is faithful in little, he will be faithful in a lot, and the idea that you cannot use worldly attitudes and methods in the kingdom.

B. Rich man and Lazarus

This parable warns that the proper use of one's wealth and blessings is to serve the needs of others, especially those who suffer. It also shows the finality of judgment once it is pronounced.

Jesus warns that His word will be the standard by which we are judged. We need to believe it. Those who saw signs as well as those who didn't will both be judged based on their obedience to Jesus' word.

103. More instructions to the disciples

Luke 17:1-10

Again Luke describes further teaching and training that Jesus gives His disciples as they travel towards Bethany. Jesus gives a serious warning to those who would make others stumble, especially children. Other subjects include teaching on being generous in forgiveness, the power of faith (mustard seed), and the duty of disciples to serve the Lord. Jesus says that these things are the natural duties of those who would be His disciples.

Much of the disciples' and Apostles' training took place during these trips.

104. Jesus raises Lazarus

John 11:17-46

Bethany was two and a half miles from Jerusalem and it has taken Jesus at least four days to get there, probably more since he is already in the tomb.

Lazarus was the brother of Mary and Martha, and Jesus stayed at their home when He was in the area. Martha meets Him before He gets to the village. She is upset because He didn't get there on time but wants reassurance her brother is saved and will resurrect in the future. Mary also met Him and is more bold in saying that He could have saved him from death had He come. She is overcome with grief.

Jesus is overwhelmed by human emotion at the death of His friend and the sorrow it has caused. With only a few words He calls Lazarus to come out of the tomb and Lazarus does so.

In Jesus' prayer we learn that the reason for the delay was to be able to perform this great miracle and glorify God through Lazarus' death. It was also done this way to provide yet another sign of His identity as Messiah.

105. The high priest decides to put Jesus to death

John 11:47-53

Some who saw the miracle were amazed and believed, others brought the news to the Jewish religious leaders. They acknowledge the great power of Jesus, but their reaction is fear that their authority and position would be challenged. They then decide to kill Him.

The king, the religious fanatics, the lawyers and now the high priest were in league to take Jesus' life. His circle of enemies was now complete.

106. Jesus retreats to the north

John 11:54

Once again Jesus avoids a situation where He could be taken before the time is right. He heads north near the border of Samaria, not quite into the region of Galilee, in a place called Ephraim.

Here He will stay and minister until the final Passover week when He will return to Jerusalem for the climax of His ministry.

Lessons

1. Jesus was focused

Note that in all this activity, travelling, threats and confrontation Jesus remained focused on one thing and one thing only: His ministry to the people. He spent little time defending Himself against His detractors or hiding out from those who wished to kill Him. Also, He did not use up time feeling sorry for Himself or being depressed. He remained "on task" every day: teaching and training the disciples, preaching to the crowds, dealing with the scribes and ministering to the people.

There will always be distractions and obstacles in our Christian lives. Despite this reality, we need to maintain our focus and stay on task in serving Jesus and the church. That is how we will cope with all of these things and find peace and satisfaction.

2. Jesus will arrive

Mary and Martha fretted over Jesus' delay. The people mourned and gave up hope. When He finally arrived, their fear and sorrow were for nothing: He raised Lazarus.

We fret and get all worked up waiting for Jesus to answer, waiting for Him to supply, waiting for Him to save us somehow, but we always worry for nothing. Whether in a little while or in the end, Jesus will always arrive and when He does He brings comfort, healing and salvation.

Let's not worry. If it's Jesus we are waiting for, He will always arrive sooner or later and when He comes He will take care of our concerns.

READING ASSIGNMENT FOR CHAPTER 10

107. Luke 17:11-19

108. Luke 17:20-37

109. Luke 18:1-14

110. Matthew 19:1-15; Mark 10:1-16; Luke 18:15-17

111. Matthew 19:16-30; Mark 10:17-31; Luke 18:18-30

112. Matthew 20:1-16

113. Matthew 20:17-19; Mark 10:32-34; Luke 18:31-34

114. Matthew 20:20-28; Mark 10:35-45

115. Matthew 20:29-34; Mark 10:46-52; Luke 18:35-19:1

116. Luke 19:2-10

117. Luke 19:11-28

118. Matthew 26:6-13; Mark 14:3-9; John 11:55-12:11

10.
3rd PASSOVER TO FINAL WEEK

In this our 10th chapter of the life of Jesus we will review the events that took place in the final phase between the third Passover and His final week. We've seen Jesus' pattern of movement as He comes into Jerusalem for the major feasts to teach and proclaim His identity with miracles and pronouncements on His deity, then retreat back to the safety of the northern region when things became too dangerous for Him in Jerusalem.

In this chapter we will look at the events that took place as Jesus was passing through the northern region one last time before entering Jerusalem to suffer His arrest and crucifixion.

Previously, the Jewish leadership had officially sanctioned His death with Caiaphas the High Priest leading the charge and so Jesus returned to the northern country for one last tour of ministry with His Apostles.

107. Jesus heals ten lepers

Luke 17:11-19

Luke specifies that Jesus was on the frontier of Samaria and on His way to Jerusalem. Ten lepers cry out to Him for mercy. They did not come near because they were not allowed to. Jesus tells them to show themselves to the priests (healed lepers had to do this to be permitted back into normal society). They all believed Him as they turned and ran towards the officials to receive their confirmation of healing. Only one (a Samaritan) turned and came to Jesus to give thanks and receives an extra, and more important blessing, forgiveness for his sins. The other 9 were like those who ate the bread and fish made by a miracle. Their bodies were nourished but their souls were untouched. The leper who returned to give thanks and pay homage to the Lord showed that the healing produced faith in Him and that faith saved his soul.

108. Prophecy concerning the end

Luke 17:20-37

The Pharisees believed that the coming of the kingdom of God would be a good thing for them. They thought that the kingdom would usher in a golden era of Jewish supremacy and they would benefit greatly as religious leaders.

With this in mind, they ask Him about the coming of the kingdom and Jesus answers them using language that was hard to discern (apocalyptic) and a message they were not prepared for:

- The kingdom was already here among them and because they missed it they were going to suffer crisis (judgment of the Son of Man).

- This crisis would come upon them suddenly and without warning.

- The crisis would bring devastation.

Of course, He is referring to the fact that He is ushering in the kingdom of God, He embodies it but they refuse to accept

Him. The result of their refusal to acknowledge Him is that they will be judged for this when He will bring judgment upon them. His warning is that they will be destroyed suddenly and only a few will escape.

This prophecy was fulfilled when the Roman army came and destroyed Jerusalem in 70 AD and only a few (Christians) managed to escape the city.

109. Parables on perseverance and pride

Luke 18:1-14

In this last ministry tour Jesus teaches in parables that deal with one's personal relationship with God:

- The parable of the widow who pesters a city official to give her justice until he gives in shows that perseverance is a powerful force even in the hands of the weak. This He taught to encourage the people to persevere in prayer to Almighty God even though they were weak and sinful. Their persevering prayers were powerful tools in appealing to God who, unlike the uncaring official, was truly interested in His peoples' concerns.

- The parable of the Publican and Pharisee shows two men praying. The Pharisee judging himself in comparison to the sinful Publican and finding himself righteous by contrast. The Publican judging himself by God's Law and finding himself guilty and unworthy. Jesus shows that God's mercy is on those who humbly acknowledge their sins, and His judgment on those who try to justify or excuse themselves.

These parables were thinly veiled rebukes of the official ruling class of religious leaders who had failed in exercising justice and mercy towards others and who had been too proud to ask for mercy from God for themselves.

110. Pharisees questions on divorce

Matthew 19:1-15; Mark 10:1-16

Jesus leaves the far northern part of the country around Galilee and heads south. He is confronted in the region of Peraea by Pharisees who wish to trap Him on the issue of divorce.

At the time there were two main schools of thought on the teaching of the Law concerning divorce found in Deuteronomy 24:1-4. The Rabbi Shammai said that "indecency" was some kind of shameful sexual behavior. The Rabbi Hillel said that "indecency" was any behavior that the husband didn't like.

The Pharisees asked Jesus, "Can a man divorce for any reason?," provoking Him to side with one or the other (N.B. at the time only men were permitted to initiate divorce). If He agreed with Shammai, they would accuse Him of being a hypocrite because He had associated with sinners and forgiven the woman caught in adultery. If He agreed with Hillel, they would accuse Him of being soft on divorce, a liberal. If He rejected both, they would accuse Him of violating the Law since the Law permitted divorce.

Jesus responds by teaching them several basic lessons about marriage that they had either overlooked or had misunderstood:

1. Marriage is a creation of God, not man. It was instituted in Genesis at the beginning and the rules

that govern it are still these: one man, one woman for life (Genesis 2:18-25).

2. The instructions in the Law permitting divorce did not change the original design of marriage. They were put there because with the arrival of sin there needed to be direction as to what to do when sin destroyed a marriage (legal divorce, no taking back original wife, protection of children, etc.). In their hard-heartedness, men were putting away their wives without any legal standing for the woman. Because of this she couldn't remarry which was her only option to support herself in that culture. Unfortunately, many women turned to prostitution or co-habitation without marriage in order to survive. Both of these situations were shameful in that society. By requiring a bill of divorce, the woman was legally free to remarry and have proper status (Deuteronomy 24:1-2).

3. What breaks the bond of marriage is a violation against the very thing that sustains that bond – sex. When there is fornication (sex sin that includes adultery, homosexuality and other forms of sexual impurity), a marriage bond is broken. Legal divorce is permissible in these cases without bringing guilt upon the innocent partner. Jesus didn't say you couldn't break the marriage bond, He said you shouldn't.

4. The ones who divorced their partners for reasons other than sex sins were guilty of several sins themselves in those days:

   o They unlawfully divorced (did what God said not to).

   o They committed adultery by breaking their marriage vows. The word adultery doesn't only refer to a sexual sin, it also means the breaking of a vow or the practice of idolatry (Jeremiah 3:9; Ezekiel 23:37; Matthew 19:9; James 4:4). Note that Jesus doesn't say, "except for fornication and marries another commits fornication" (which specifically refers to sexual sin); He says, "commits adultery."

o They caused their innocent partners to be stigmatized as adulterers in the eyes of society (because all would assume that this was the true reason they were put away). Or even caused them to sexual sin (prostitution).

o They caused even the future mates to be stigmatized as adulterers by society for the same reason.

Pharisees were notorious for their many divorces and Jesus doesn't permit them to justify themselves by claiming they had "legal" divorces. He shows them that the Law that governs marriage is in Genesis and demonstrates the extent of the damage they did when they divorced. There is further teaching on marriage and divorce in I Corinthians that we will not cover here.

It is after this confrontation that Jesus stops to bless the little children brought to Him, and warns the Apostles and everyone not to hinder children to come to Him for blessings.

Innocence and trusting faith was important to succeed in marriage as well as entering into the kingdom.

111. The rich young ruler

Matthew 19:16-30; Mark 10:17-31; Luke 18:18-30

The rich young ruler represents what was best about the Jewish nation. He was young, wealthy, knowledgeable of the Law and pious in that he tried to carefully obey it. The result of this, however, simply brought him to the point where he realized that something was missing. He wanted eternal life and confessed that with all his trying, he had not yet grasped it. Jesus tells him that to get "eternal" life, he must leave his "temporal" life (money and position) and follow Him. At his meeting with the Lord, the young man found out that his great love of wealth was standing in the way of his eternal life. Jesus takes the opportunity here to warn about the danger of wealth and how its pursuit can blind and block a person's ability to see or enter into the spiritual kingdom.

Peter at this point complains that the Apostles have already given up their wealth to follow Jesus and the Lord reassures Peter that their reward will far outweigh what they've given up for Him. In the kingdom, the first (rich and powerful) are last, and the last (humble and weak) first.

112. Parable of the laborers in the vineyard

Matthew 20:1-16

In line with His warning about riches and services, Jesus also teaches about attitude by telling the parable of the workers hired at different times of day for the same pay.

In this parable He shows that whatever we receive from the Lord: it is always fair, it is always generous and it is not based on our deserving work but on His kindness.

This is one of the three occasions where Jesus uses the saying: The first shall be last and the last first. Other passages: response to Peter and Apostles about their reward for following Him (Matthew 19:30), response to a question regarding who will be saved (Luke 13:30).

113. Jesus predicts His death/resurrection a third time

Matthew 20:17-19; Mark 10:32-34; Luke 18:31-34

Jesus once again predicts His death and resurrection, but this time gives more details in the manner of His suffering and death as well as a clear indication of His resurrection three days later.

Luke says that even at this late date, the Apostles still did not understand what He was talking about.

114. James and John's request

Matthew 20:20-28; Mark 10:35-45

Sensing that the time of an important event is near (the coming of an earthly kingdom with the Apostles at the head), James and John make a bid for choice positions in the new order. This would be to sit at the right and left of the throne. This upsets the others who resent their grab for power.

Jesus answers that they have not and will not suffer in a way to deserve this (He will), that they will however suffer because of the kingdom and gain their request (sit with church at right hand of God in Christ), the high position they seek is obtained through service and humility in the kingdom and not by jockeying for power.

115. Jesus heals two blind men

Matthew 20:29-34; Mark 10:46-52; Luke 18:35-19:1

In the review of the three accounts, we see that one of the two blind men was named Bartimaeus, and he was the one who called out to Jesus by proclaiming Him as Messiah (Son of David). Both were encouraged to not bother Jesus, but the Lord answered their call and healed their blindness.

The name of one of the blind men, Bartimaeus, suggests that he became a well known member of the Jerusalem church.

116. Jesus goes to Zaccheus' house

Luke 19:2-10

The miracle of healing the blind men occurred as Jesus was entering Jericho (northeast of Jerusalem). After this miracle the crowds followed Him as He went through the city. One person in the crowd was the chief tax collector for that place. His name was Zaccheus. Being short, he climbed a tree to see Him go by. Jesus spotted him and said He would eat with him. Zaccheus was probably the most despised man in the city and least worthy to receive Jesus, but when the opportunity came he gladly received Jesus into his home.

While eating, Zaccheus is so overwhelmed with gratitude that he publically repents of his sins and commits himself to doing right and Jesus forgives and blesses him then and there.

117. The parable of the minas (pounds)

Luke 19:11-28

During this same dinner the question of when the kingdom would arrive comes up again. The Jews continually asked this question because they were anxious for their version of the kingdom to arrive since they felt ready for it and it would benefit them.

Jesus responds with the parable of the minas/pounds (a measure of money, equals roughly $25 today). The parable is similar to the one in Matthew about talents but is a different parable told to a different audience.

In the story the rebellious subjects refuse to submit to a nobleman while he is away. When he returns, he punishes them. While he is away he leaves his 10 slaves with money to invest and, like the parable of the talents, the ones who succeed are rewarded and the ones who were lazy or afraid lose the little they had to begin with.

The point for the Jews was that they had been both rebellious and unprofitable and were about to be punished by losing what they had.

118. Mary anoints Jesus with perfume

Matthew 26:6-13; Mark 14:3-9; John 11:55-12:11

Jesus leaves Jericho and moves closer to Jerusalem by going to Bethany for a dinner in His honor at the home of Simon the Leper (probably the one healed by Jesus). Simon was connected to Lazarus, Mary and Martha somehow (perhaps the father) since they were at his house also and the women were serving food. There were crowds around the house looking to see Lazarus whom Jesus had raised from the dead. It was a final meal with friends and supporters, and while eating Mary uses expensive perfume to anoint Jesus' head as a way of honoring Him.

When the others complain (Judas) about the cost and waste, Jesus tells them that this is a preparation for His death and Mary will always be remembered for it.

Meanwhile, dark clouds are forming around the Lord as the chief priests were plotting to seize Him and Lazarus (according to John 12:9-10) and put them to death since too many people were now beginning to follow Jesus.

In the next chapter we will begin to review the events occurring during Jesus' last week before His death.

Lessons

1. God deals with man based on need, not merit

Note that the Jews were continually rebuked by Jesus because they came to God with their culture, achievements, self-righteousness. However, the ones received and blessed by the Lord were those who were aware of their weaknesses and came to God with a need for righteousness, forgiveness, mercy; and they were satisfied.

2. Don't waste an opportunity to be with Jesus

The blind men, Zaccheus, Simon the Leper – all took advantage of the time to be with the Lord, even the crowds. We should count it a privilege, not a problem for those times we can be with our Lord at worship or Bible study, prayer, service, etc. Don't pass up the opportunity when it comes by. Those who spend time with Him now will be with Him later.

READING ASSIGNMENT FOR CHAPTER 11

119. Matthew 21:1-11; 17; Mark 11:1-11; Luke 19:29-44; John 12:12-19

120. Matthew 21:12-19; Mark 11:12-19; Luke 19:45-46

121. Matthew 21:21-22; Mark 11:20-26

122. Matthew 21:23-22:14; Mark 11:27-12:12

123. Matthew 22:15-23:39; Mark 12:13-40; Luke 20:20-47

124. Mark 12:41-44; Luke 21:1-4

125. John 12:20-36

126. Matthew 24:1-42; Mark 13:1-37; Luke 21:5-36

127. Matthew 24:43-25:46

128. Matthew 26:1-5; 14-16; Mark 14:1-2; 10-11; Luke 22:1-6; John 12:36-50

11.

LAST PASSOVER TO CRUCIFIXION WEEK

We are entering into the sixth section in our outline – last Passover to the crucifixion.

In the last chapter we saw the Lord making His way from the northern countryside one final time, teaching and performing miracles along the way. The last scene was at Simon the Leper's home with Lazarus, Martha and Mary along with His Apostles sharing a fellowship meal. This meal was eaten in Bethany, only a few miles from Jerusalem and the powerful enemies that awaited Him there.

This section is divided into six days.

Sunday – April 2nd

119. Jesus' triumphant entry

Matthew 21:1-11; 17; Mark 11:1-11; Luke 19:29-44; John 12:12-19

Most who came to Jerusalem for Passover were pilgrims who would normally walk. Jesus sends His Apostles to get a donkey for Him to ride on as was prophesied of in Isaiah 62:11; Zechariah 9:9. This was to show not only His divine Messianic role, but also the humility of the Christ (a worldly savior that the Jews were hoping for would have come in on a horse).

The crowds cry out Hosanna ("Oh save" Psalms 118:25, expression of adoration) and lay out cloaks and branches as a mark of respect and honor. The crowds were excited. Once He arrives at the temple there is no welcoming committee, no honor for Him, no belief from the leaders.

He mourns over the judgment coming upon the city and nation because of this and returns to Bethany to spend the night.

Monday – April 3rd

120. Jesus curses the fig tree / cleanses the temple

Matthew 21:12-19; Mark 11:12-19; Luke 19:45-46

Jesus cursing the fig tree after He had come to it and it had no figs to offer Him is a living parable that reflects what has taken place when Jesus came to Jerusalem and its people, but they had nothing to offer Him (faith and praise). Just as the fig tree will wither and die, so will the nation.

On the second visit Jesus chases the merchants and animals out of the temple. This was the second time He did this. The first was at the beginning of His ministry, the second at the end of it.

Once again He returns to Bethany for the night.

Tuesday – April 4th

121. Lesson on the withered fig tree

Matthew 21:21-22; Mark 11:20-26

Jesus returns to the temple the next day with His disciples and they pass by the cursed fig tree and see that it has completely withered overnight. Jesus' lesson on this is that with faith all things are possible. The alteration of nature is not too hard for Him – whether it's withering a tree or casting a mountain into the sea – both are equally easy for Him. What unleashes spiritual power however, is faith and if the Apostles have faith, they will do even greater things.

We know that they did do these greater things because later on they saw Jesus resurrect and themselves performed mighty miracles – even raised people from the dead.

122. Jesus teaches in the temple

Matthew 21:23-22:14; Mark 11:27-12:12

It was the Passover week and there were large crowds in Jerusalem. Jesus' teachings were bound to stir up the people so the Jewish leaders try to neutralize Him by confronting Him. They challenge His authority to cast out the money changers and His reply is to ask them what they believed concerning John the Baptist.

Remember, these confrontations were staged in front of the crowds so the leaders were sensitive to what the crowds heard. As far as John was concerned, if they said he was a prophet Jesus would ask them why they didn't obey Him. If they rejected John openly, the crowds would reject them because they believed he was a prophet. In the end, they said nothing and claimed ignorance.

To this response Jesus tells them three parables.

1. Parable of two sons

A father asks two sons to do something. One says yes but doesn't do it, the other says no but changes his mind and obeys the father.

The point of the parable was to show that the Jewish leaders were charged with a duty that they accepted but didn't fulfill, and those that had previously disobeyed and neglected the task (sinners and Gentiles) would one day obey the Father in their place.

2. Parable of the landowner

Jesus describes wicked vine growers who refuse to pay their dues to the landowner. They would reject or kill all those who would come to collect the rent, even the landowner's son. Finally, Jesus predicts that the landowner will eventually come and punish them. Again, the target and meaning is quite obvious.

3. Parable of marriage feast

A king prepares a feast but none of the guests want to come, they even beat and kill the messengers sent to invite them. The king destroys these and in order to have the wedding feast for his son, he invites the poor and homeless to be his guests, to wear the wedding guest garments and enjoy the feast. One refuses to wear the offered garment and is cast out of the feast.

Of course the parables were directed at the religious leaders who now were being publicly rebuked by Jesus for their disbelief in Him as Messiah. As a result they desire to kill Him.

123. Jesus responds to questions

Matthew 22:15-23:39; Mark 12:13-40; Luke 20:20-47

While at the temple many come to Him with questions and challenges.

1. Pharisees and Herodians concerning taxes

Once the Priests have failed to destroy His credibility the Pharisees along with the Herodians (a group that supported Herod's position as king and feared that Jesus' teachings would upset his delicate hold on power), tried to challenge Him by asking Him if it was in accordance with God's law to pay taxes to Caesar.

This unpopular tax (poll tax) was a token of the Jews' subject status under Rome. If Jesus said yes, He would alienate His followers who hated the Roman authority. If He said no, they would accuse Him of insurrection.

Jesus simply answers that the tax belongs to Caesar (his face was on the coinage) and giving it to him was no offense to God because it belonged to him. But the Lord clarified that what belonged to God must also be rendered unto Him as well. Jesus implies here that what belongs to God, however, should not be given to Caesar, and vice versa which sets the limits of where human government leaves off and divine authority continues.

2. Sadducees concerning resurrection

The previous question was political in nature, the next is theological. Sadducees did not believe in resurrection or angels. They rejected miracles and did not accept the books of prophets as authoritative. They only held to the Pentateuch for their authority (Genesis, Exodus, Leviticus, Numbers, Deuteronomy). They present Jesus with a foolish story about 7 brothers each marrying the same woman and ask Jesus which man's wife will she be in heaven. The question was meant to mock the idea of the resurrection.

Jesus shows that their disbelief and errors were based on the misunderstanding of the very text they accepted. He showed that in Exodus 3:6 God referred to Himself as the one who cared for men who were long dead. This meant that these men continued to exist before Him in some form. This proved the concept of life after death from their own text! (I AM the God of Abraham…)

He also gives them an insight that only God would know: that men don't have wives in heaven because they are like angels in nature (spiritual). Not only does He answer their question on their own terms but He reveals their ignorance in doing so.

3. Lawyer's question on the greatest command

Pious Jews often repeated the Shema (Deuteronomy 6:4-5): "Hear O Israel, the Lord is our God, The Lord is One! And you shall love the Lord your God with all your heart and with all your soul and with all your might."

When a lawyer asks Jesus what the greatest commandment is, the Lord repeats the Shema, but adds to this a companion verse in Leviticus 19:18: "You shall love your neighbor as yourself." He does this to show that loving God is not only demonstrated in ceremony and temple worship (which was important also), but in a very real way acted out as love towards others. Our love towards God has an impact on the world only when we love others in His name.

The lawyer agrees with Jesus and the Lord tells him that he is not far from the kingdom (what was missing of course was faith in Him as Messiah).

4. Jesus asks them a question

After His adversaries have asked their questions, He asks them a question concerning the Scriptures and what they teach about the Messiah. Their concept of the Messiah was that he would be a descendant of the great king David and, much like David, would bring the nation to political and economic greatness. Jesus corrects this idea by showing them from Scripture that David himself described the Messiah as a divine being coming in the form of a man through David's lineage. (Psalm 110:1: The Lord said to my Lord).

The Jews understood the implications of this (that Jesus claimed not only to be the Messiah, but the Divine Messiah) and were silenced, not venturing to say another word.

5. Jesus' last warning

Once He has finished teaching and responding to them, Jesus rebukes the priests, Pharisees and scribes. He reviles them for their pride (wanting the honor of men instead of God), hypocrisy (don't do what they teach), legalism (no grace of God in their teachings) and disbelief (killed the prophets sent by God). He condemns them and mourns over the city that has rejected Him, and because of this will suffer destruction.

124. The widow's offering

Mark 12:41-44; Luke 21:1-4

Of course not all Jews were like the leaders: greedy, unbelieving and proud. Jesus commends the love and generosity of a poor widow who gives all she had as an offering in order to show her faith and trust in God. This scene is described to show the tremendous difference between the humble and acceptable servant of God (who had little but gave a lot) and those rejected by God (who were given much but returned nothing).

125. Some Greeks desire to see Jesus

John 12:20-36

The final group to come seeking Jesus were Greek converts to Judaism who had little respect among the Jews. Their eagerness to see and hear Him prompts Jesus to offer a prayer in which He:

- Predicts His death again and the fruit it will bear as He is resurrected.

- Hears a voice from heaven answering His prayer to glorify the Father's name.

- Encourages the crowd to believe and warns them of the consequences for not doing so.

After addressing the general crowd He leaves the temple area once again.

126. Jesus prophesizes concerning the destruction of Jerusalem and the end of the world

Matthew 24:1-42; Mark 13:1-37; Luke 21:5-36

Jesus brings Peter, James, John and Andrew with Him outside the city to teach them about the things that will come. In these long passages Jesus talks about an event in the near future (the end of the Jewish nation with the destruction of the city and temple by the Romans – 70 AD) as well as an event in the distant future which would be the end of the world at His second coming.

There are some who interpret these passages as exclusively end of the world scenarios, however, Jesus specifically mentions that these things would happen to the present generation in Matthew 24:34.

It is helpful if we realize that this passage has 3 historical viewpoints:

1. A panorama of world history that includes the present time when Jesus is speaking, the near future referring to the destruction of Jerusalem in 70 AD, and the end of the world at Jesus' return. (vs. 4-14)

2. Jesus telescopes to events leading to the destruction of Jerusalem in 70 AD. (vs. 15-35)

3. He telescopes again to his second coming at the end of the world. (vs. 36-42)

All this is done to prepare His disciples for the near (70 AD) and distant (end of the world) future.

127. The last parables

Matthew 24:43-25:46

Having given His final teachings and warnings to the Jews along with the preparation of His Apostles concerning the end of the Jewish state, Jesus goes on to tell them parables concerning the following people.

1. The good man and the house
2. The wise and evil servants
3. The ten virgins
4. The talents
5. The sheep and goats

All of these have a similar theme: that one does not know when the judgment is coming but must be ready at all times for final judgment.

Wednesday – April 5th

As the sun sets, Jesus is on the Mount of Olives teaching and preparing His Apostles for what is to come. Officially, the next day begins after this and so as the following day emerges we see the Lord continuing to teach and train His Apostles.

128. Judas plots to betray Jesus

Matthew 26:1-5; 14-16; Mark 14:1-2; 10-11; Luke 22:1-6;
John 12:36-50

Of course, after their stinging rebuke, the Jewish leaders agree to kill Jesus as soon as the Passover is complete (avoid crowd reaction and riots). Judas plays into their hands by coming to them at this precise moment with a plan to betray the Lord, and they agree to pay. In the meantime, the writers say that the crowds were still undecided as to who they believed Jesus was. Many leaders believed but were afraid to acknowledge this openly. Jesus pronounces judgment on all of these by saying that His words will judge them in the end (meaning how they reacted to His teaching will judge them before God).

Lessons

1. There will be an end

The Jewish leaders refused to believe that there would be an end to their nation as Jesus predicted. History shows that they were terribly and tragically mistaken. Jesus has also predicted the end of our world and how to be ready for that. Let's learn from their mistake and believe Jesus when He warns us about this.

2. His Word will judge

Parents won't judge, Law won't judge, our conscience won't judge; the final judge will be the New Testament. How we react to Jesus' words will determine what happens to us in the end. The sheep will be the ones who followed Jesus' words, the goats will be the ones who didn't think they were important or worth believing and obeying.

Our Bible study is not simply an exercise in learning, it is also an act of preparation for the end.

READING ASSIGNMENT FOR CHAPTER 12

129. Matthew 26:17-19; Mark 14:12-16; Luke 22:7-13

130. Matthew 26:20-25; 31-35; Mark 14:17-21; 27-31;
Luke 22:14; 21-38; John 13:1-38

131. Matthew 26:26-29; Mark 14:22-25; Luke 22:15-20

132. John 14:1-17:26

133. Matthew 26:30; 36-56; Mark 14:26; 32-52;
Luke 22:39-53; John 18:1-12

134. Matthew 26:57-68; Mark 14:53-72; Luke 22:54-71;
John 18:13-27

135. Matthew 27:1-2;11-30; Mark 15:1-19; Luke 23:1-25;
John 18:28-19:16

136. Matthew 27:3-10

137. Matthew 27:31-44; Mark 15:20-32; Luke 23:26-38;
John 19:16-22

138. Matthew 27:45-61; Mark 15:33-47; Luke 23:39-56;
John 19:23-42

139. Matthew 27:62-66

12.
LAST PASSOVER TO CRUCIFIXION WEEK CONTINUED

We are reviewing the events that took place in the sixth section entitled "Last Passover and Crucifixion Week." In the last chapter Jesus has come to Jerusalem and confronted all of the religious leaders there. They have rejected Him and He has pronounced judgment on them and the nation of Israel by describing the events that will take place when Jerusalem will be destroyed some forty years into the future. The last scene sees Judas plotting with the Jewish leadership to betray Jesus into their hands.

We've divided these final events into the different days of that last week. So far we have looked at the events that took place from Sunday to Wednesday. In this chapter we pick up the story on Thursday morning as Jesus prepares for the Passover meal.

Thursday – April 6th

129. Disciples sent to prepare Passover meal

Matthew 26:17-19; Mark 14:12-16; Luke 22:7-13

The Passover meal was coming on the following day (which would begin that evening). Jesus sends Peter and John to go ahead and prepare the meal. He tells them that they are to go into the city and they will find a man carrying water (easy to spot since women usually did this work) and this person would lead them to the room where they were to prepare the feast. Preparing meant to provide the lamb sacrificed at the temple and meat cooked, unleavened bread, bitter herbs (cucumber, lettuce in bitter dressing), wine, as well as cushions, cups, plates, water and towels for the foot washing courtesy. Jesus knew they would find the man. Some say He had prepared in advance but the text suggests that the Lord used His divine knowledge to prepare all of this.

Friday – April 7th

130. Jesus eats the Passover with Apostles

Matthew 26:20-25; 31-35; Mark 14:17-21;27-31;
Luke 22:14; 21-38; John 13:1-38

Each gospel writer describes this key event and each places some details in different order. Matthew and John were there so in combining their accounts this seems to be the way it took place on that night.

- Jesus gathers the twelve in the upper room in order to celebrate the Passover.

- Peter and John had set up the dinner and had taken their places nearest to Jesus. As a result a dispute breaks out as to who is the greatest.

  - Jesus tells them that the greatest are those who serve and He promises them that they will be in the kingdom.

- After this teaching He takes the water and towel set up for foot washing and washes all of their feet, including Judas'.

  o The water and the towel were used by a slave to wash guests' feet.

  o None of the Apostles wanted to lower themselves to render this courtesy to one another.

  o Jesus does so in order to demonstrate His point about servanthood.

- After taking His place at the table, He indicates that there is a betrayer among them.

  o He shows Peter and John who this is by offering Judas a piece of bread dipped into the bitter herbs.

  o After this, Judas leaves the room.

- After Judas leaves, Jesus prays for the Apostles and what they will do after His death.

  o He prays for Peter to be safe from Satan's attacks.

  o He foretells their abandonment of Him and how He will restore them.

  o He tells them that He will meet them again in Galilee.

All of these things take place as they are sharing the traditional Passover meal.

131. Jesus initiates the Lord's Supper

Matthew 26:26-29; Mark 14:22-25; Luke 22:15-20

During the time of Jesus the Jews would eat the Passover in the following way:

- The meat represented the sacrifice slain on their behalf.

- The bitter herbs represented their bitter experience in Egypt.

- The unleavened bread represented the haste in which they left.

- The wine represented two things: the blood shed in Egypt and the good life in the Promised Land.

- The leader of the household would offer prayers, eat and drink the 4 cups of wine and others would follow his lead.

- At some point a child would ask why they did this and the leader would retell the story of the Jewish exodus from Egypt.

Jesus served as leader and led them through the meal. Once the food was gone and there remained only one piece of unleavened bread and the final cup of wine to drink, He changed the significance of the meal.

- From now on the bread would represent His body offered up for sin.

- From now on the wine would represent His blood shed to obtain life for sinners.

This memorial meal would no longer remember the Jews' freedom from Egyptian bondage, it would now commemorate their own personal freedom from the bondage of sin, because of His body and blood.

132. Farewell address and prayer

John 14:1-17:26

This is the longest uninterrupted passage where Jesus speaks that is contained in the New Testament.

This long prayer and exhortation was given while they were standing (John 14:31) in the upper room. In it He covers many things:

- An assurance that He is the way to heaven and He will prepare a place for them.

- A guarantee that their requests to God in His name will be answered.

- A promise of the coming of the Holy Spirit to comfort and teach them.

- An exhortation to remain faithful and fruitful and draw strength from Him as a branch draws from the vine.

- A warning of future persecutions.

- An explanation of what the Holy Spirit will do for and in them when He comes (convict, comfort, inspire).

- An encouragement not to quit when they are rejected by the world, that He will be with them and give them peace (at this point they all confess their faith in Him).

- A prayer to God on their behalf so that God will unite, protect and glorify Himself through them.

Once He finishes this long discourse they sing the Hallel (Psalms 115-118) and depart from the upper room.

133. The agony and betrayal in the garden

Matthew 26:30; 36-56; Mark 14:26; 32-52; Luke 22:39-53;
John 18:1-12

The Mount of Olives on the east side of Jerusalem was covered with olive trees and had an olive press where the oil was made (Gethsemane=olive press).

Jesus takes His Apostles there to pray with Him during His final hours. He brings Peter, James and John more deeply into the garden and then finds Himself a secluded spot to pray. Three times He returns to find the Apostles sleeping while He agonized in prayer concerning what was to take place.

His final prayer is so intense He sweats blood and eventually accepts (His human nature does) the will of the Lord for His crucifixion. In the meantime Judas has organized a mob of people to come and seize Him, which he does by kissing Jesus to indicate which of the men they were to arrest. Peter lobs off the ear of one of the men there (Malchus) and Luke says Jesus healed Him (His last miracle). The mob takes Him away while the Apostles scatter to their safety. Peter and John follow the mob to see what will happen.

134. Jesus before the High Priest

Matthew 26:57-68; Mark 14:53-72; Luke 22:54-71;
John 18:13-27

At first Jesus is brought before Annas, Caiaphas the High Priest's father. Eventually a council is convened in the middle of the night with the High Priest presiding.

In the meantime, Peter (and some think John) have worked their way into the courtyard and is challenged there as a disciple of the prisoner, Jesus, which he denies vehemently three times (just as Jesus told him).

During this "trial" (illegal because it was at night) witnesses are brought forward to accuse Jesus but their testimony is contradictory. Finally the High Priest asks Jesus directly and the Lord acknowledges His divine identity. Based on this confession the High Priest condemns Jesus to death for blasphemy and they begin to slap and taunt Him.

135. Jesus before Pilate and Herod

Matthew 27:1-2; 11-30; Mark 15:1-19; Luke 23:1-25; John 18:28-19:16

The Jews were not allowed to execute anyone so they had to convince the Roman officials that a prisoner was worthy of death. Pilate was the Roman Proconsul and he controlled the province with Roman soldiers. He appointed the High Priest, controlled the treasury and even maintained the vestments of the High Priest (releasing them for festivals).

Jesus' appearances before Pilate occurred in the following way:

- The Jews bring Jesus accusing Him and demanding His death. Pilate questions Him and then sends Him to Herod.

- Herod tries to get Jesus to do a miracle for him and when this fails he sends Him back to Pilate.

- Pilate questions Jesus again not finding any basis for execution and tries to free Jesus under the tradition of freeing a prisoner at the Passover, but the crowd chooses to free Barabbas instead of Jesus.

- Pilate's wife warns him against condemning Jesus, but he gives in to the pressure of the crowd and turns Jesus over to the soldiers for execution.

- Once sentenced, the soldiers begin to torture Jesus, humiliate Him and prepare Him for His execution.

136. Judas' suicide

Matthew 27:3-10

After seeing what has happened, Judas is stricken with guilt because he has betrayed an innocent man. He still doesn't believe in Jesus as Messiah, only that Jesus is innocent. He returns the money and hangs himself in despair.

137. Jesus is crucified

Matthew 27:31-44; Mark 15:20-32; Luke 23:26-38; John 19:16-22

Jesus carries His own cross (with help from Simon of Cyrene) to the place of execution, Golgotha (the skull). He is offered drugged wine to enable them to crucify Him without resistance, but He refuses. He is crucified between two thieves as they and the crowd mock and challenge Him to save Himself.

Once He is secured with nails and hoisted in an upright position, He asks the Father to forgive His tormentors. The Romans put a sign above His head that says "king of the Jews" which the Jewish leaders object to.

138. Jesus dies on the cross

Matthew 27:45-61; Mark 15:33-47; Luke 23:39-56;
John 19:23-42

It's amazing how each writer provides an enormous amount of detail as to what happened during the few hours Jesus was on the cross:

- One of the thieves repents of what he has said and asks Jesus to save him, which the Lord does by promising that he will be in paradise.
- The soldiers gamble for and divide His clothes.
- Jesus gives to John the charge to keep His mother.
- Jesus was crucified at 9 AM and from noon to 3 PM the sky was darkened.
- Jesus cries out to God not to forsake Him.
- He said that He was thirsty.
- He declares that His mission is complete by saying, "It is finished."
- He dies by offering up His life in the words, "Father, into Thy hands I commit my spirit."
- At this point the veil in the temple at the entrance of the Holy of Holies was torn in two and many who were dead came out of their tombs (but only after His resurrection).
- There was an earthquake and because of these signs, even the centurion at the foot of the cross believed.

Once He died, the soldiers pierced His side to make sure and the process of burial began.

- Joseph of Arimathea comes to claim the body from Pilate and along with Nicodemus they wrap Jesus' body and place it into a new tomb belonging to Joseph.

- Mary Magdalene and Mary (mother of Joses), who was Jesus' mother's sister (the Lord's aunt), remained by the tomb until sunset and the beginning of the Sabbath.

Their goal was to properly prepare the body for burial, but with the sunset and Sabbath beginning they couldn't do this and so planned to return on the Sunday to finish their task.

Saturday – April 7th

The Lord is buried, the crowds are disbursed, but the Jews are still trying to make sure that His influence is extinguished.

139. Pilate sets a seal on the tomb

Matthew 27:62-66

The Jewish leaders were afraid that Jesus' followers would steal the body and claim resurrection to keep their movement alive. Pilate not only puts a seal on the entrance to the tomb to avoid tampering, but also permits the Jews to add guards to foil any attempt to try to remove the body.

Lessons

For this chapter I make one important observation rather than practical lessons from the material we have covered.

1. Keep the main thing the main thing

Writers spent more time writing about the events that covered a few hours of Jesus' death and resurrection than all of the three years of ministry. The Holy Spirit makes this the central event in our religion. If this is so then we need to remember to:

- Understand and teach this as our central doctrine (death and resurrection of Christ to save mankind) and not get sidetracked by issues.

- Give greater importance to sharing the communion each week because it represents the central issue of our spiritual lives.

We must not only speak where the Bible speaks, we must also emphasize what the Bible emphasizes.

READING ASSIGNMENT FOR CHAPTER 13

140. Matthew 28:2-4

141. Matthew 28:1; Mark 16:1-4; Luke 24:1-3; John 20:1-2

142. Matthew 28:5-7; Mark 16:5-8; Luke 24:4-8

143. Mark 16:11; Luke 24:12; John 20:3-10

144. Mark 16:9; John 20:11-18

145. Matthew 28:8-10

146. Matthew 28:11-15

147. Luke 24:34

148. Mark 16:12-13; Luke 24:13-35

149. Luke 24:36-49; John 20:19-23

150. Mark 16:14; John 20:24-31

151. Matthew 28:16-20; Mark 16:15-18

152. John 21:1-25

153. I Corinthians 15:6-8

154. Mark 16:19-20; Luke 24:50-53

13.
RESURRECTION / APPEARANCES / ASCENSION

In this last chapter we will cover the events of the seventh period of Jesus' life that include His resurrection, appearances and final ascension.

In the previous section we saw the Jewish leaders demanding and obtaining permission to post a guard at Jesus' tomb in order to prevent any tampering by His disciples. We also learned that the female disciples intended to return to the grave after the Sabbath in order to properly prepare Jesus' body for final rest.

The Final Forty Days

There are three main events that took place after the death and burial of Jesus. Each scene is described by several gospel writers.

A. The Resurrection

140. The resurrection itself

Matthew 28:2-4

Only Matthew described what actually took place before the women arrived that morning to find an empty grave.

- There was a severe earthquake.
- This coincided with the descent of an angel.
- He rolled the stone away from the entrance and sat upon it.
- The soldiers guarding the tomb fainted.
- The angel's appearance was like lightning and his clothing was white.

We are not told how Jesus left the tomb or if He said anything, only the angel's appearance and the guards' reaction (they fainted and did not see the Lord because He showed Himself only to believers after His resurrection).

141. The women find the empty tomb

Matthew 28:1; Mark 16:1-4; Luke 24:1-3; John 20:1-2

Mary Magdalene, Jesus' Aunt Mary, Johana and others come to the tomb to finish the burial process. They find it open and empty. By now the soldiers have run back to the chief officials. Mary Magdalene immediately returns to tell the Apostles leaving the other women alone at the graveside.

142. The angels speak to the women

Matthew 28:5-7; Mark 16:5-8; Luke 24:4-8

The women who remain see two angels and also become afraid. They invite the women to inspect the tomb and tell them to go and tell the disciples what has taken place, all according to what was promised. They also tell the women that Jesus has gone to Galilee (in the north again) to meet His disciples. These women also leave with the intention of telling the disciples that the Lord has risen from the dead.

143. Peter and John arrive at the tomb

Mark 16:11; Luke 24:12; John 20:3-10

Now that the other women have left the scene to tell the Apostles and disciples, Peter and John arrive. They have been told of the resurrection by Mary Magdalene, and while the others were skeptical, Peter and John have raced to the scene ahead of Mary who is trailing behind.

John arrives first but waits for Peter to go inside. Once inside they see the linen wrappings on the ground and the towel, used to cover his face, rolled up in the corner. John says that once they saw the empty tomb, they then believed and understood what Jesus had been telling them concerning His resurrection.

B. The Appearances

These are very hard to put in order because of the small time frame and little background information given.

144. Appearance #1 – Mary Magdalene

Mark 16:9; John 20:11-18

After Peter and John have seen the empty tomb and left, Mary Magdalene arrives once again at the scene. The Bible says that she does see two angels sitting in the tomb who ask her why she is weeping. When she goes outside she sees Jesus who she mistakens for the gardener at first and she asks Him where they have taken the body.

When Jesus speaks, she recognizes Him and tries to cling to Him, but Jesus does not permit it. He sends her to tell the Apostles of His resurrection and imminent ascension.

145. Appearance #2 – Other women

Matthew 28:8-10

The other women, who had seen the angels and were en route to the city were now visited by the resurrected Christ while on their way. Matthew reports that the women took hold of His feet and worshipped Him and He told them what the angels had said: go tell the disciples that He would meet them in Galilee.

146. The priests bribe the guards

Matthew 28:11-15

While all of this is going on with Jesus' disciples, Matthew reports that the guards who had fainted at the appearance of the angels have gone to their superiors to tell them what had happened. They are in trouble since it was their duty to guard the tomb, so the Jewish leaders arrange to pay them a bribe to claim that the body was stolen while they slept. They agree in exchange for the promise that if this came to the attention of Pilate, the priests would vouch for them. Matthew claimed that this was the "official" story given out at the time that he wrote his gospel some 30-40 years after the fact (Matthew – 60-70 AD).

147. Appearance #3 – Peter

Luke 24:34

Peter doesn't even mention this appearance in his own writings. One of the men who had seen the Lord on the road to Emmaus recounts that the Lord told them that Jesus had indeed appeared to Simon Peter. Paul confirms this fact in I Corinthians 15:5 with a similar reference.

148. Appearance #4 – Two disciples on the road to Emmaus

Mark 16:12-13; Luke 24:13-35

We no longer know where Emmaus was located, but it was near Jerusalem (5-7 miles).

The two disciples were on their way home after being witnesses of what happened to Jesus in Jerusalem. While discussing this, Jesus comes along and begins to travel with them sharing in their conversation. They are prevented from recognizing Him as He questions them regarding their discussions.

- They tell Him that they were hoping that Jesus would have been the Messiah, but now that He has been tortured and killed, they're not so sure.

- Like most Jews, they hoped the Messiah would be a glorious figure like David (warrior king).

- In the Old Testament, Isaiah (53:1-12) presented the Messiah as a figure of suffering and servanthood. Many Jews saw this as a personification of themselves – even to this day.

- Jesus comes to these two disciples and explains to them that the Messiah would have two profiles:

1. A suffering servant

It wasn't the Jews who were Isaiah's model for his suffering servant – it was the Messiah that he was talking about. Jesus' suffering was not a repudiation of His claim as Messiah, it was a confirmation that He truly was fulfilling all that was written about Him in the Old Testament. This was a stumbling block for Jews and Jesus explains this to these two disciples.

2. A glorious Savior

Like David who saved his people, Jesus in His resurrection defeats man's greatest enemy: death.

This was the nature of what Jesus taught these two disciples along the road. As darkness approached, they invite Him to spend the night with them and as they ate and Jesus blessed the meal, they recognize Him and He disappears from their sight. They return to Jerusalem to report this to the Apostles.

149. Appearance #5 – Jesus appears to the Apostles and disciples

Luke 24:36-49; John 20:19-23

When the two disciples find the Apostles and begin telling them of their experience, Jesus suddenly appears among them. At this first appearance among them, the Apostles were frightened and He reassures them by showing His hands and feet and asks for something to eat. After this, He teaches them what He had taught the two disciples along the road – that according to the Scriptures the Messiah had to suffer, die and resurrect. What they were seeing was the true fulfillment of scripture.

John tells us that it is at this point that Jesus breathes on them and gives them the gift of the Holy Spirit (they received John's baptism and were justified at that point). Now they receive the indwelling of the Spirit to permit their growth in Christ (sanctification).

Today we receive both at the point of baptism (Acts 2:38).

After this Jesus gives them the charge to be His witnesses in preaching the gospel, but to wait in Jerusalem until they receive the empowering from the Holy Spirit.

150. Appearance #6 – Thomas

Mark 16:14; John 20:24-31

In the previous appearance to the Apostles, Thomas was not among them, but this time he is. Mark says that Jesus rebuked them for being hard-hearted and unbelieving. John gives a fuller description of the scene where Jesus appears with the greeting, "Peace be with you" and takes special care in convincing Thomas of His person. Thomas acknowledges Jesus as Lord and God, and Jesus (this may be the rebuke Mark refers to) says that they have believed because they have seen but blessed are they who will believe without seeing. John comments that these things have been recorded for the express purpose of helping those who haven't seen to believe.

151. Appearance #7 – The Great Commission

Matthew 28:16-20; Mark 16:15-18

Jesus sends the Apostles north into Galilee where the majority of His ministry had taken place. It is here that He gives them the charge to go into all the world to preach, baptize and teach. His time for departure is drawing near so He comforts them with the promise that He will always be with them.

152. Appearance #8 – At the Sea of Galilee

John 21:1-25

John gives another long description of a time when Jesus appears to Peter and the other Apostles as they were fishing. It is here that Peter is reconciled with the Lord over his denial (Jesus asks for his love 3 times) and here Jesus gives him back his apostolic ministry (feed my sheep).

There is an explanation by John as to why some in the 1st century believed that he would not die until Jesus returned, but John says that Jesus merely stated that if He wanted Him to remain alive until that time that was His decision to make, no one else's. It didn't mean that he would live until then, only that Jesus could do this if He wanted to.

He completes this chapter with the same kind of editorial comment that the record he kept only contained part of the things Jesus did – enough to generate faith, but if all were written it would fill the world.

153. Appearance #9 – Non-Gospel

I Corinthians 15:6-8

Not all of Jesus' appearances were recorded in the gospels. Paul also describes some of Jesus' appearances that fit into the gospel narrative, but are not included by the writers. Simply for sequence sake we note that Jesus appeared to over 500 in Galilee (perhaps when He gave the great commission).

He also appeared to James (His earthly brother) and Paul the Apostle, but this was much later after His Ascension.

Approximately 549 people recorded seeing Him in different situations and on different days.

C. The Ascension

The final great event recorded by the gospel writers is the ascension of Jesus back into heaven.

154. The ascension

Mark 16:19-20; Luke 24:50-53

Luke says that this took place in Bethany, a place of happy memories with the Apostles, disciples and friends. They watched Him ascend into heaven as He blessed them.

Together, Mark and Luke record that the Apostles felt great joy, returned to Jerusalem, and later on preached the good news. Luke gives a more complete version of this event in the first chapter of the book of Acts where he explains that the Lord instructed them to remain in Jerusalem to await the baptism with the Holy Spirit which would empower them to do miracles and preach.

In His final words to them, He repeated the charge to be His witnesses to the world and Luke says that two angels encouraged them to stop looking into the sky noting that He would return some day in the very same way.

Lesson

This is our last chapter and I want to share one last lesson or thought on this series.

1. We are mentioned

Even though Jesus' words were directed mostly toward the Apostles, their situation and the work that was ahead of them – Jesus also referred to us directly.

In John 20, when He tells Thomas and the others that their faith was based on what they had seen, but blessed would be those whose faith would come even though they had not actually seen – that's you and I He's talking about.

I always envied those whose names were actually mentioned in the Bible (David, Peter, Lydia, etc.) and how secure they must have felt because their names were recorded in the inspired text.

Well, in His kindness, Jesus has made room for all of us in the phrase "Blessed are they who did not see, and yet believed." Every time you read that passage realize that your name is included there from Jesus' own lips, and take heart – for He will return one day to call your name in order to be with Him in heaven forever. This is possible because even though you have not seen, through His word, you have believed.

BibleTalk.tv is an Internet Mission Work.

We provide textual Bible teaching material on our website and mobile apps for free. We enable churches and individuals all over the world to have access to high quality Bible materials for personal growth, group study or for teaching in their classes.

The goal of this mission work is to spread the gospel to the greatest number of people using the latest technology available. For the first time in history it is becoming possible to preach the gospel to the entire world at once. BibleTalk.tv is an effort to preach the gospel to all nations every day until Jesus returns.

The Choctaw Church of Christ in Oklahoma City is the sponsoring congregation for this work and provides the recording facilities and oversight. If you wish to support this work please contact us at the address below.

bibletalk.tv/support

Made in the USA
Las Vegas, NV
25 August 2023